Raspberry Pi Home Automation with Arduino

Second Edition

Unleash the power of the most popular microboards to build convenient, useful, and fun home automation projects

Andrew K. Dennis

[PACKT] open source*

PUBLISHING

community experience distilled

BIRMINGHAM - MUMBAI

Raspberry Pi Home Automation with Arduino
Second Edition

First published: February 2013

Second edition: February 2015

Production reference: 1200215

Published by Packt Publishing Ltd.
Livery Place
35 Livery Street
Birmingham B3 2PB, UK.

ISBN 978-1-78439-920-7

www.packtpub.com

Credits

Author
Andrew K. Dennis

Reviewers
Ed Baker

Rémy Bétus

Piotr Kula

Commissioning Editor
Akram Hussain

Acquisition Editor
Richard Brookes-Bland

Content Development Editor
Prachi Bisht

Technical Editor
Mitali Somaiya

Copy Editor
Vikrant Phadke

Project Coordinator
Shipra Chawhan

Proofreaders
Simran Bhogal

Chris Smith

Indexer
Mariammal Chettiyar

Production Coordinator
Melwyn D'sa

Cover Work
Melwyn D'sa

About the Author

Andrew K. Dennis is the manager of professional services software development at Prometheus Research. This company is a leading provider of integrated data management for research, and is the home of HTSQL, an open source navigational query language for RDBMS.

Andrew has a diploma in computing and a BS in software engineering. He is currently studying for a second BS in creative computing.

He has over 10 years of experience in the software industry in the UK, Canada, and USA. His experience includes Python and JavaScript development, e-learning, CMS and LMS development, SCORM consultancy, web development in a variety of languages, open source application development, and a blog dedicated to maker culture and home automation.

His interests include web development, e-learning, 3D printing, Linux, the Raspberry Pi and Arduino, open source projects, parallel computing, home automation, amateur electronics, home networking, and software engineering.

Many of these topics were covered in his previous book, *Raspberry Pi Super Cluster, Packt Publishing*.

I would like to thank my wife, Megen, for supporting me throughout this project, and my parents for their support with my interest in technology while I was growing up.

I would also like to thank the team at Prometheus Research for making this a great and interesting place to work and helping to change the face of data management.

Finally, I would like to thank everyone who bought the first edition of this book, and the team at Packt Publishing for commissioning this second edition.

About the Reviewers

Ed Baker graduated with a BSc in Physics from Imperial College in 2007, and somehow ended up working in the Entomology Department of The Natural History Museum shortly afterwards. His work focuses on how technology (both hardware and software), can improve the way research is performed, from field data collection to final publication. Outside the technology world, he is fond of stick insects, cockroaches, and grasshoppers.

Recently, Ed's work has focused on automated acoustic and environmental monitoring and protocols for sensor networks. He has started a biodiversity technology company called Infocology.co.uk.

Ed's first book, provisionally titled *Arduino for Biologists*, will be published in 2015 with Pelagic Publishing.

I would like to thank Philippa for believing that writing and tinkering would bring rewards in the end.

Rémy Bétus is a web developer in e-commerce, and he integrates open source solutions. He's always been an enthusiast on the Arduino, the Raspberry Pi, and other DIY products. He was also a member of the Fablab in his engineering school, where he discovered all of these wonderful things. He is also passionate about development, networks, telecommunication, and science in general.

www.PacktPub.com

Support files, eBooks, discount offers, and more

For support files and downloads related to your book, please visit www.PacktPub.com.

Did you know that Packt offers eBook versions of every book published, with PDF and ePub files available? You can upgrade to the eBook version at www.PacktPub.com and as a print book customer, you are entitled to a discount on the eBook copy. Get in touch with us at service@packtpub.com for more details.

At www.PacktPub.com, you can also read a collection of free technical articles, sign up for a range of free newsletters and receive exclusive discounts and offers on Packt books and eBooks.

https://www2.packtpub.com/books/subscription/packtlib

Do you need instant solutions to your IT questions? PacktLib is Packt's online digital book library. Here, you can search, access, and read Packt's entire library of books.

Why subscribe?

- Fully searchable across every book published by Packt
- Copy and paste, print, and bookmark content
- On demand and accessible via a web browser

Free access for Packt account holders

If you have an account with Packt at www.PacktPub.com, you can use this to access PacktLib today and view 9 entirely free books. Simply use your login credentials for immediate access.

Table of Contents

Preface

The world of home automation is an exciting field that has exploded over the past few years with many new technologies in both the commercial and open source worlds. This book provides a gateway for those interested in learning more about this topic and building their own projects.

With the introduction of the Raspberry Pi computer in 2012, a small and powerful tool is now available for the home automation enthusiast, programmer, and electronic hobbyist. It allows them to augment their home with sensors and software.

Combining Raspberry Pi with the power of the open-hardware Arduino platform, this book will take you through several projects in which you will build electronic sensors, and introduce you to software that will record their data for later use.

We hope you will enjoy the second edition of *Raspberry Pi Home Automation with Arduino*.

What this book covers

Chapter1, An Introduction to the Raspberry Pi, Arduino, and Home Automation, introduces the technologies used in the book and provides a conceptual background to the world of home automation.

Chapter 2, Getting Started – Setting Up Your Raspberry Pi and Arduino, is a guide to your Raspberry Pi, Arduino, and the Cooking Hacks Raspberry Pi to Arduino bridge shield.

Chapter 3, Central Air and Heating Thermostat, teaches you how to build a thermostat using the Arduino platform to control your central air conditioning and heating.

Chapter 4, Temperature Storage – Setting Up a Database to Store Your Results, shows you how to build a database to store your projects' data, and explore it via your web browser.

Chapter 5, Parcel Delivery Detector, demonstrates a system using Arduino and Raspberry Pi that will alert you whenever a parcel arrives at your door.

Chapter 6, Curtain Automation – Open and Close the Curtains Based on the Ambient Light, teaches you how to integrate motors with your projects to open and close blinds and curtains using the skills learned in previous chapters.

Chapter 7, Water/Damp Detection – Check for Damp/Flooding in Sheds and Basements, helps you build systems that can check for humidity and water to indicate dampness and flooding.

Chapter 8, Wrapping Up, finishes the topic with some ideas for future projects.

Appendix, References, lists a collection of links to the resources used in this book and other interesting information.

What you need for this book

- Raspberry Pi (version B+)
- A SD card
- Ardunio Uno
- A Seeed Ethernet shield
- Cooking Hacks' Raspberry Pi to Arduino bridge shield
- An Arduino motor shield
- A Pololu relay module
- An AM2302 combined thermistor/humidity sensor
- An LED
- A Seeed Grove Water sensor
- A 10K ohm resistor
- A force resistor sensor
- A 9V or 12V DC motor
- A breadboard
- Breadboard wires and power supply
- USB cables
- A Cat-5 Ethernet cable
- An Internet connection with a home modem or router
- A small electric fan

- A small wooden disc to wrap blind cords around
- Soldering iron or a gun with solder (optional)
- A Windows, Mac, or Linux-based machine (optional)
- A television or monitor with HDMI or S-video (optional)
- A USB keyboard, USB mouse, cables for S-Video to HDMI conversion, and sponges (all of these are optional)
- Tweezers and cable strippers (optional)

Who this book is for

If you are new to Raspberry Pi, Arduino, or home automation, and you wish to develop some amazing projects using these tools, then this book is for you. Any experience in using the Linux operating system or Raspberry Pi will be an added advantage.

This book is a step-by-step guide that will help you in setting up components and software in each chapter.

Conventions

In this book, you will find a number of styles of text that distinguish between different kinds of information. Here are some examples of these styles, and explanations of their meanings.

Code words in text, database table names, folder names, filenames, file extensions, pathnames, dummy URLs, user input, and Twitter handles are shown as follows: "Once logged in, we are going to run apt-get to install SQLite3."

A block of code is set as follows:

```
#!/usr/bin/env python
import sqlite3
import urllib2
import json
```

Any command-line input or output is written as follows:

```
cd ~
mkdir database
cd database
```

New terms and **important words** are shown in bold. Words that you see on the screen, for example, in menus or dialog boxes, appear in the text like this: "If you see the **Getting darker** message, try shining your flashlight on the sensor."

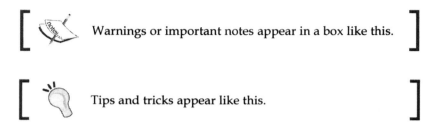

Warnings or important notes appear in a box like this.

Tips and tricks appear like this.

Reader feedback

Feedback from our readers is always welcome. Let us know what you think about this book—what you liked or may have disliked. Reader feedback is important for us to develop titles that you really get the most out of.

To send us general feedback, simply send an e-mail to feedback@packtpub.com, and mention the book title via the subject of your message.

If there is a topic that you have expertise in and you are interested in either writing or contributing to a book, see our author guide on www.packtpub.com/authors.

Customer support

Now that you are the proud owner of a Packt book, we have a number of things to help you to get the most from your purchase.

Downloading the example code

You can download the example code files for all Packt books you have purchased from your account at http://www.packtpub.com. If you purchased this book elsewhere, you can visit http://www.packtpub.com/support and register to have the files e-mailed directly to you.

Errata

Although we have taken every care to ensure the accuracy of our content, mistakes do happen. If you find a mistake in one of our books—maybe a mistake in the text or the code—we would be grateful if you could report this to us. By doing so, you can save other readers from frustration and help us improve subsequent versions of this book. If you find any errata, please report them by visiting http://www.packtpub. com/submit-errata, selecting your book, clicking on the **Errata Submission Form** link, and entering the details of your errata. Once your errata are verified, your submission will be accepted and the errata will be uploaded to our website or added to any list of existing errata under the Errata section of that title.

To view the previously submitted errata, go to https://www.packtpub.com/books/content/support and enter the name of the book in the search field. The required information will appear under the **Errata** section.

Piracy

Piracy of copyright material on the Internet is an ongoing problem across all media. At Packt, we take the protection of our copyright and licenses very seriously. If you come across any illegal copies of our works, in any form, on the Internet, please provide us with the location address or website name immediately so that we can pursue a remedy.

Please contact us at copyright@packtpub.com with a link to the suspected pirated material.

We appreciate your help in protecting our authors, and our ability to bring you valuable content.

Questions

You can contact us at questions@packtpub.com if you are having a problem with any aspect of the book, and we will do our best to address it.

1
An Introduction to the Raspberry Pi, Arduino, and Home Automation

This chapter provides an introduction to the Raspberry Pi, Arduino, Arduino to Raspberry Pi connection bridge, and the subject of home automation.

We'll look at the history of the Raspberry Pi and how it came to being, as well as the Arduino platform, an open source microcontroller that provides developers with a means to interact with their surroundings through a variety of sensors and motors.

Next, we will explore the Arduino to Raspberry Pi connection bridge, a method of attaching an Arduino shield to the Raspberry Pi. We will wrap up the chapter by covering home automation and how technologies such as the Raspberry Pi have put the ability to build complex sensor-based systems in the hands of the open source community.

First, let's start by looking at what we will be covering in the coming chapters of this book. We have a number of exciting projects ahead that will slowly introduce home automation via technologies such as Raspberry Pi and Arduino. These projects include:

- Writing software to control hardware
- Building a thermometer using a thermistor
- Turning the thermometer into a thermostat using relays
- Controlling electric motors using a motor shield
- Writing software to store sensor data generated by your projects

As you go through each chapter in this book, you will gain a basic knowledge of building circuits and hardware for home automation projects. You will then learn to write software to both control your hardware projects and record the data generated by them. Finally, we will consider future projects that you can build with your newly acquired skills.

Our next step is to learn a little about the background of the technologies that we are going to use. We will start with the Raspberry Pi.

History and background of the Raspberry Pi

From the first vacuum tube computers to the tape and punch card machines of the 1960s and the first microprocessor mainframes of the 1970s, computing had very much been the preserve of large businesses and the research departments of universities. However, by the late 1970s, with the release of Apple II and seeds planted earlier by technologies such as the TV Typewriter and Apple I, this was rapidly changing.

By the 1980s, the public could buy low-cost home computers, such as the ZX Spectrum and Commodore 64, which hit the market and subsequently gave birth to a whole generation of amateur programmers. By the 1990s, these programmers, brought up on tinkering with their home computers and writing BASIC, were heading to academia and the computer industry, and helping to forge the dot-com boom with game, web, and business technologies.

The genesis of the Raspberry Pi is linked to this in many ways. A group of computer scientists led by Eben Upton at the University of Cambridge's computer laboratory in 2006 struck upon the idea of producing a cheap, educational microcomputer geared towards amateur computer enthusiasts, budding students, and children. The aim was to help provide the skills for future computer science undergraduate applicants that many of the applicants in the 1990s possessed. This was largely because home computers of the 1980s required programming and were open to hacking.

However, it would be another two years before the project became viable, and until 2012 before the Raspberry Pi was being shipped to the public.

The 2000s saw a huge growth in mobile computing technologies, a large segment of which was being driven by the mobile phone industry. By 2005, ARM—a British designer of CPU core components and by-product of the 1980s' home computer company Acorn—had grown to a state where 98 percent of mobile phones were using their technology. This translated into around 1 billion CPU cores. ARM technology later ended up featuring on the Raspberry Pi, with the ARM1176JZF-S processor core being used as a part of the Broadcom BCM2835 **System-on-a-Chip (SoC)**.

During the same period, Eben Upton designed several concepts for the Raspberry Pi, and by 2008, thanks to a by-product of the increasing penetration of mobile phone technology, the cost of building a miniature, portable microcomputer, with many of the multimedia functions that the public was accustomed to, was becoming viable. Thus, the Raspberry Pi Foundation was formed to develop and manufacture the Raspberry Pi computer.

By 2011, the first Alpha Models were being produced and tested, and the public finally got to see what the Raspberry Pi was capable of. Demos of Quake III Arena and full HD 1080px video showed that the tiny computer could pack a big punch for low cost.

Finally in 2012, the Raspberry Pi was ready for public consumption. Two versions of the Raspberry Pi were manufactured, namely Model A and Model B, with B being released first.

Over the subsequent years, both A and B were upgraded, with the Models A+ and B+ being release and this was complemented with the introduction of the Raspberry Pi 2 in 2015.

For the projects in this book, you will need to use at least a Model B version of the board, or the more powerful Model B+ or Raspberry Pi 2 Model B if available.

Next, let's learn about the Arduino platform.

History and background of the Arduino

One of the most popular open-hardware products to have hit the market is the Arduino platform. Developed in Italy by Massimo Banzi and David Cuartielles in 2005, Arduino is an open-hardware technology coupled with a programming language and an **Integrated Development Environment (IDE)** based on the open source wiring software.

The Arduino platform allows the user to create custom hardware and applications that control it via its namesake programming language. Cheap and easy to use, Arduino is an alternative to expensive programmable cards and closed commercial systems. Therefore, it helped pave the way for home enthusiasts to build their own home automation projects.

Currently, there are several board models in the market with a wide range of sizes and components; for example, the Lily Pad allows enthusiasts to attach an Arduino board to clothing for textile-based electronic projects. These boards support a wide range of shields—Arduino-compatible electronic boards that can be plugged into it and expand its functionality. One particular extension has been the introduction of Ethernet shields and wireless XBee devices that allow communication with home networks and the Web. What makes Arduino suitable for amateur enthusiasts is that little or no knowledge of how electronic components are soldered is required to use its prebuilt shields. As the user becomes more comfortable with the technology, they can progress to building their own projects using the numerous kits and sensors available on the market.

This easy adoption has helped contribute to a number of websites and books dedicated to home automation projects that use this technology.

Throughout the following chapters, you will explore the use of Arduino alongside the Raspberry Pi. For the projects in this book, we recommend using the Uno board pictured as follows:

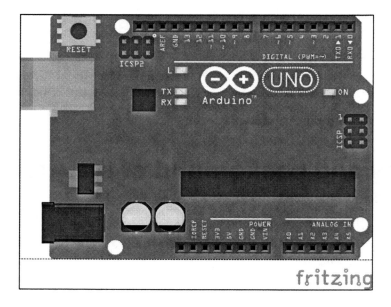

You can read more about Arduino products at `http://arduino.cc/en/Products.Compare`.

Next, we shall look at the Raspberry Pi to Arduino connection bridge, a method of connecting your Arduino shields to your Raspberry Pi.

Raspberry Pi to Arduino shield connection bridge

For two of the projects in this book, we will be using the Raspberry Pi to Arduino shield connection bridge. This is produced by Cooking Hacks, an offshoot of the Libelium wireless communications company based in Spain.

 Their website can be found at `http://www.cooking-hacks.com`.

By connecting this device to our Raspberry Pi, we get to reuse our Arduino shields and components, and get the power and storage of the Raspberry Pi running behind it. This opens up many options for complex home automation projects that may need to host databases or run memory-intensive software.

The Cooking Hacks shield is connected to the Raspberry Pi's **General Purpose Input/Output (GPIO)** pins. With the inclusion of the arduPi software, you will be able to communicate between your electronic devices, the Raspberry Pi's operating system, and web-based projects.

The Cooking Hacks shield should look like this:

Image courtesy: Cooking Hacks

A wide range of Arduino shields can be used with the connection bridge. At the time of writing this book, the Arduino shield connection bridge was available for €40.

Many of these shields can be found on the Arduino website at `http://arduino.cc/en/Main/Products`.

The shields specifications can be also be found at `http://www.cooking-hacks.com/documentation/tutorials/raspberry-pi-to-arduino-shields-connection-bridge`.

By learning to use this shield, you will discover how you can extend the functionality of your Raspberry Pi so that it can mimic the Arduino microcontroller and reuse components from other Arduino projects that you may have attempted in the past or will build in the future.

Soldering

Soldering is the process of attaching electronic components using a heated metal filler (the solder), in order to allow electrical current to flow between them.

At this point, it is worth mentioning that practicing some soldering before you start building the projects in this book is worth the effort, but not strictly necessary. If you are a novice, do not worry because there will be minimal soldering.

Also, if you have any old PC hardware sitting around, such as a graphics card that is no longer in use, you can practice desoldering and resoldering the components until you become comfortable with the process. This will also help you to get used to the soldering iron and desoldering tool.

Creating software for the Arduino

After you have set up the Arduino microcontroller and Arduino shield, and plugged it into the Raspberry Pi, you will probably be wondering how to interact with it. After all, it has sensors and LEDs, but these are nothing without applications to control them in a meaningful manner.

There are many software languages available for building projects with, but we are interested in the Arduino programming language, C++, Python, SQL, and HTSQL.

- The Arduino programming language is a subset of C++ and provides us with a tool to program the Arduino microcontroller, Arduino-compatible shields, and the components connected to them. One benefit of using this technology is that there is a wealth of programs and libraries online that can be used for future projects. You will be using this language in the Arduino IDE and on the Raspberry Pi to write the core applications that will be reading data from sensors attached to your projects.

- The next language that we will be using is Python. Python is a high-level programming language developed in the late 1980s by Guido Van Rossum named after the popular comedy show Monty Python's Flying Circus. This language allows you to build web and database applications that can be used to process the output of Arduino programs. We will be using Python to build a web application that can process data sent to it and then insert it via SQL into a SQLite3 database.

- We will also be using SQL to build the database that our Python script connects to. In conjunction with the SQLite database management system, we will construct a repository to store some of the results from our projects, for example temperature data.

- Besides these languages, we will also be using **Hyper Text Structured Query Language (HTSQL)** to provide a web interface to our database that is easy to access via the web browser and query via HTTP.

Now that we have looked at our tools to build home automation systems, the Raspberry Pi and Arduino, let's look at what home automation is.

What is home automation?

Having picked up this book, you may already have an idea of what home automation is, but just in case you don't, we'll give you a brief overview of the subject and the open source technology that is driving many projects out there today.

Home automation is more than just a remote control for your TV. Examples include programming your DVD to record your favorite shows, setting the AC unit to turn on when the temperature reaches 76 degrees Fahrenheit, and installing a fancy alarm system that contacts the police in case of a break-in.

Also known as domotics (a portmanteau between domestic and informatics), home automation can be summed up as a mechanism of removing as much human interaction as technically possible and desirable in various domestic processes, and replacing it with programmed electronic systems. It is essentially automation of home activities.

History of home automation

Concepts for home and building automation were around for decades before becoming a reality, and were featured in the writing of the 19th century science-fiction author H. G. Wells, comics, and cartoons such as The Jetsons. American industrialist George Westinghouse helped to pioneer the AC electrical system, which the X10 home automation standard would later run on, and in 1966, the company that bears his name, Westinghouse Electric, employed an engineer who developed what could arguably be called the first computerized home automation system — ECHO IV.

The **Electronic Computing Home Operator (ECHO)** was featured in the April 1968 edition of *Popular Mechanics* and had been expanded from a set of spare electronics, both in the physical sense and the literal sense, to include computing its founder Jim Sutherland's family household finances and storing their shopping lists, amid an array of other tasks.

You can still read the original *Popular Mechanics* article online, at
`http://books.google.com/books?id=AtQDAAAAMBAJ&pg=PA7`
`7&source=gbs_toc_r&cad=2#v=onepage&q&f=false`.

The ECHO never went commercial, and through the 1960s, hobbyists and a number of large companies such as Honeywell toyed with the idea of computerizing homes. However, it was the 1970s, much as with personal computing, that saw the birth of the modern era of home automation technology.

X10 – a standard is born

The introduction of the X10 technology standard can be arguably described as the beginning of modern home automation technology. Conceived in 1975 by Pico Electronics, who later partnered with Birmingham Sound Reproducers, X10 laid out the framework to allow remote-controlled access of domestic appliances. The X10 standard was designed to allow transmitters and receivers to work over existing electrical wiring systems by broadcasting messages such as "turn off" and "turn on" via radio frequency bursts.

In 1978, X10 products began to make their way into stores, geared towards electronics enthusiasts, and shortly after, in the 1980s, the CP-290 computer interface made its way to the market for the Mattel Aquarius computer.

The CP-290 unit allowed computers to communicate with X10-compatible home appliances. Over the years, support for Windows and Mac was included, and it gave those interested in home automation the ability to program their lighting systems, thermostats, and garage doors from their home computers.

As revolutionary as X10 has been, it unfortunately has a number of flaws. These include:

- Wiring and interference issues
- Commands getting lost in transmission
- Limited scope of products supporting X10
- Limited scope of commands available
- Slow speed of signal transmission
- Lack of encryption
- Lack of confirmation messages without expensive two-way devices

By the late 1990s, home automation still hadn't penetrated the home market on a truly wide scale. However, the technological advancements of the dot-com boom were providing a whole new set of tools, protocols, and standards that addressed many of the flaws of the X10 standard.

The dot-com boom and open source – a new set of technologies

With the explosion of technologies that followed the birth of the Web in the 1990s, home computing and networking technologies were now available to the public and could be easily and cheaply installed at home. These technologies would later provide an ideal candidate to push the boundaries of what could be achieved by home automation enthusiasts, and provide the industry with the tools to build smart home appliances and systems. It was only a small step from PC-to-PC communication to appliance-to-PC communication.

Home networks running on Ethernet, and later on Wi-Fi, provided a mechanism that could allow computers and electronic appliances to communicate with one another across a home without needing to use the existing electrical wiring. In the case of Wi-Fi, no extra cabling was required.

As protocols such as FTP and HTTP became the norm to access information across the Internet, hardware developers saw the opportunity to leverage these communication technologies in open source hardware devices. While X10 appliances had no way of knowing whether a signal had been successfully sent without the purchase of costly two-way devices, web technologies provided a whole framework to return error codes and messages.

At approximately the same time when the Arduino platform was being developed, the first tablet computers were beginning to be released. From 2005 until now, there has been an explosion in mobile, tablet, and smartphone devices. This growth has been commonly referenced to as the post-PC era.

These devices have provided mobile computing platforms that can run complex software and be small enough to fit in the user's pocket. As a result of this, applications that allow the user to control consumer electronics, such as the TV, have been developed for the iPhone and Android.

Due to their size, portability, and low cost in some cases, they have provided the perfect platform to interface with home appliances and devices, and provided an extension to a medium the user is familiar with.

Alongside the explosion in hardware, there was an equivalent explosion in software. One particular product of interest that we will look at is the open source Android operating system.

Android OS is a Linux-based operating system geared towards mobile devices. As a part of the Open Handset Alliance—a consortium of 84 companies operating in the mobile sphere—Google backed and eventually purchased the Android mobile operating system. The aim has been to create an open source operating system that can compete with companies such as Apple, and provide a robust system that can work across multiple manufacturers' devices.

As a result of this, commercial manufacturers of home appliances have begun to embed the technology and software into their products, and a generation of smart devices has started to appear in stores around the world.

Commercial products

If you are interested in a smart refrigerator that can tell you the weather and keep track of your groceries, or an oven that can be controlled via your smartphone, then you are in luck. Products such as the Samsung RF4289HARS refrigerator running Android and the LG smart washing machine are paving the way for smart homes by embracing open source and web-based technologies. It is also not just appliances that are getting the makeover. Firms such as the Nest—a company founded by ex-employees of Apple—are developing smart thermostats.

Barcodes and QR codes on products now allow the consumer to scan them with their smartphones and download information about the item directly from the web. This can be extended to allow scanning and inventory management of products at home, recording data such as consumption dates of products in the refrigerator, and dynamically generating shopping lists.

This combination of hardware, software, and information now provides the potential for the home to become a part of "the Internet of Things" as quoted by Kevin Ashton.

Thanks to open source and open standard technology being used in these devices, it is easy to combine home-brewed projects built with the Raspberry Pi and commercial products by companies such as LG to build a smart home with a network of devices that can communicate with one another to combine the execution of tasks.

As we mentioned, home-brewed systems such as the Raspberry Pi can form part of this network. Let's now look at the effects of the arrival of the Raspberry Pi on the world of home automation.

Arrival of the Raspberry Pi

With the arrival of the Raspberry Pi and the Raspberry Pi to Arduino shield, there is now a set of open source technologies that combine the power of a PC, the communication and multimedia technologies of the Web, the ability to interact with the environment of a microcontroller, and the portability of a mobile device.

Coupled with the existing Arduino microcontrollers, we have the perfect set of tools to allow us to build cheap devices and systems for our homes. These devices can then interface with their commercial counterparts and can also be tailored for our own needs, while providing great tools to learn about technology.

For those familiar with the Arduino platform, the Raspberry Pi combined with its shields provides an all-in-one medium to create devices without the need for a separate PC or Mac—giving us an alternative to solutions that currently exist.

The ability of the Arduino Uno to communicate with the Raspberry Pi via an Ethernet shield over a LAN gives us flexibility in the types of projects that we can build. You will see this in the coming chapters where an Arduino Uno writes information back to a Raspberry Pi that is hosting a database.

Also, thanks to the Raspberry Pi's mission of providing an educational tool for those interested in programming, the addition of the Arduino shield will provide a mechanism for those who wish to move from writing software that manipulates the Raspberry Pi to software that manipulates their environment and provides a pathway to learn about electronics. This could have the positive effect of bolstering the ranks of Homebrew and Maker clubs with an eye towards home automation, and lead to an ever-increasing diversity of tools being produced for the public.

Summary

In this chapter, we provided an overview of the Raspberry Pi and Arduino platform. We also looked at some of the existing technologies used in home automation and their history. While Sutherland's ECHO IV filled a room in his house, the Raspberry Pi occupies space not much larger than a credit card.

Home automation now seems to be taking the next step to becoming widely adopted, and the Raspberry Pi neatly fits into this world by providing those who want to customize control of their devices with an easy and a cheap tool to achieve it, and also by expanding what can be done with Arduino technology currently out in the marketplace.

With this in mind, we will get started on our first project—setting up the Raspberry Pi. Here, we will install the necessary software to get our Raspberry Pi up and running, and install the Arduino IDE so that we can program our Arduino Uno.

2
Getting Started – Setting Up Your Raspberry Pi and Arduino

This chapter aims to provide a quick overview on setting up the Raspberry Pi and Arduino. In order to use your Raspberry Pi, you need to start by installing an operating system on an SD card. Once this is in place, you can install extra software to write code.

Setting the up Arduino is much simpler. All you need is to download the IDE and plug the Arduino into your computer via a USB cable. We will start this chapter by walking through the Raspberry Pi setup.

The SD card – our Raspberry Pi's storage device

A **secure digital (SD)** card is a form of a portable, high-performance storage medium available for electronic devices ranging from cameras to PCs.

The Raspberry Pi comes equipped with an SD card slot, allowing us to insert an SD card and use it as our device's main storage mechanism, much like a hard disk on a PC. While you can use other storage mechanisms such as a USB drive or USB external hard drive, the SD card is small and thus lends itself better to embedded devices such as those found in home automation projects.

There are various brands of SD cards in the market, and they come in a wide range of sizes. The Raspberry Pi supports larger SD cards such as those with 64 GB of storage space. For the projects in this book, you should be using a card with a minimum of 2 GB storage.

The official Raspberry Pi website provides a handy guide to SD cards, at `http://www.raspberrypi.org/documentation/installation/sd-cards.md`.

We will now look at the options available with regards to purchasing an SD card preinstalled with an operating system, and then we will learn how to format and install it ourselves.

Preinstalled SD card versus a blank SD card

Since the Raspberry Pi was released, a number of websites have been offering preloaded SD cards that come installed with one of the operating systems that are available for the Raspberry Pi. These are a good option for amateur enthusiasts looking to get started with the Raspberry Pi, who do not want to go through the setup process and are happy with a single, preloaded operating system.

The official Raspberry Pi store sells a preinstalled card. You can find it at `http://swag.raspberrypi.org/products/noobs-8gb-sd-card`, preinstalled with **New Out Of the Box Software (Noobs)**.

Another option is to purchase a blank SD card and follow the instructions in this chapter.

With this in mind though, if you do not have a home PC or Mac to use in order to format a blank SD card, we recommend purchasing a preformatted card. This should come loaded with the Debian Wheezy Raspbian OS, as this is the version of Linux we will be using throughout the book.

A note on Noobs

Noobs is an operating system installation manager that you can add to your SD card. It makes the setup of your Raspberry Pi simple and provides you with an option to try out different operating systems.

If you decide to try out Noobs, we recommend selecting Raspbian in order to follow along with the examples in this book.

The Raspberry Pi website provides an introduction and guide to Noobs at `http://www.raspberrypi.org/help/noobs-setup/`. You can also download Noobs from `http://www.raspberrypi.org/downloads/`.

If you have not installed Raspbian via Noobs, then keep reading. Otherwise, you can jump directly to the *Raspberry Pi SSH setup* section later in this chapter.

Downloading Raspbian

The download links for the Raspbian operating system can be found on the Raspberry Pi download page, at `http://www.raspberrypi.org/downloads/`.

There are a couple of options with regards to the method of downloading this file: over a torrent or as a ZIP file.

Once the file is downloaded, you can move on to the steps to set up the SD card and install the operating system.

Setting up the SD card and installing Raspbian

Installing an operating system is a two-step process. This involves formatting the SD card to the FAT filesystem format, and copying and pasting the image to the card.

File Allocation Table (FAT) is a method used for recording which sectors of a disk files are stored in and which sectors are free to be written to. It has its origins in the 1970s, when Bill Gates and Marc McDonald developed it for use on floppy disks. Due to its robustness and simplicity, it is still found on SD cards today and is the format we will need in order to install Raspbian.

When you purchase an SD card, you might notice that it is already formatted to FAT, as this format is popular with devices such as digital cameras. Many manufacturers ship the card so that it is ready to go out of the box and no further formatting is required. However, we recommend formatting your card if you did not purchase the official SD card.

To format and copy the downloaded Raspbian image to your card, follow the official steps at the Raspberry Pi website, depending on your operating system:

- **Linux**: http://www.raspberrypi.org/documentation/installation/installing-images/linux.md
- **Mac OS X**: http://www.raspberrypi.org/documentation/installation/installing-images/mac.md
- **Windows**: http://www.raspberrypi.org/documentation/installation/installing-images/windows.md

Once the operating system is installed, we can wrap up its configuration by ensuring that the **Secure Shell (SSH)** for remote connection to the Raspberry Pi is up and running.

Raspberry Pi SSH setup

You have now successfully completed the Raspberry Pi setup and will see the Raspbian Linux desktop. This desktop contains a number of icons that will load the programs installed by default, including Midori, a fast and light web browser, and the Python programming language IDE (**integrated development environment**), both of which we will be using.

Also of note is the LXTerminal. This icon launches the Linux Terminal window, which allows us to run applications via the command line.

A final task that we can complete before moving on to installing our Arduino software is to check whether SSH is up and running. We will be using SSH to connect to our Raspberry Pi remotely in future projects. Perform the following steps to set up SSH:

1. Open a Terminal window and type the following command:

   ```
   ps aux | grep sshd
   ```

2. You should see the following process running:

   ```
   root      2067  0.0  0.2   6208  1060 ?        Ss   18:17   0:00 /
   usr/sbin/sshd
   ```

3. If you do not see the SSH process running, enter the following command:

   ```
   sudo /etc/init.d/ssh start
   ```

After this command has run, try running the previous command again and check whether the sshd process is present. We will learn about this in detail in *Chapter 4, Temperature Storage – Setting Up a Database to Store Your Results*.

[You can use the ps command to show running processes on your Raspberry Pi.]

With this task complete, let's move on to installing the software we need to program the Arduino.

Arduino

Our first task is to install the Arduino IDE. The Arduino IDE is where we will write the code and upload it to the microcontroller.

[This piece of software can be found at http://arduino.cc/en/main/software.]

Here, you will find the installation instructions for your operating system, including Linux, Windows, and Mac OS X. It is also possible to install the Arduino IDE directly on the Raspberry Pi. The following instructions will provide an overview of this process.

Installing the IDE on your Raspberry Pi

If you wish to install the IDE directly on your Raspberry Pi, you can do this via the command line. This will be necessary if you don't have a second computer on which you can install the Arduino IDE.

Once you have the Terminal window open, type the following command:

```
sudo apt-get install arduino
```

Accept any prompt that appears on the screen. The installation takes up about 81 MB of space.

Now that the installation is complete, you will be able to open the Arduino IDE on your Raspberry Pi and connect your microcontroller directly to the Raspberry Pi's USB drive.

A quick guide to the Arduino IDE

The Arduino IDE is a graphical user interface that allows you to develop Arduino code and then upload it directly to the microcontroller.

When you launch the program, you will be presented with a sketch. This is where you will write your Arduino code:

1. You will find a number of options in the top menu. These include the examples that come bundled with the Arduino IDE, which can be found by navigating to **File | Examples**.

2. Try selecting this option **0.1 Basics | BareMinimum**.

3. To upload an example to your microcontroller, ensure that it is plugged in. Next you will need to set the board. You can do this by navigating to **Tools | Board**. Here, you will find a list of the Arduino microcontrollers, and then you can select the model you have purchased, for example, Arduino Uno.

4. Next, we need to select the USB port that the board is plugged into so that the IDE knows where to upload the sketch code.

 If your Arduino IDE does not detect the USB port, you may need to run the application as root via sudo. StackExchange provides some suggestions on fixing this issue, at http://arduino. stackexchange.com/questions/739/arduino-program- only-works-when-run-as-root.

The USB port list can be found by navigating to **Tools | Serial Port**.

Once you have the serial port correctly configured, you can upload the code to the microcontroller.

5. Click on the play button icon in the sketch. If everything was configured successfully, your code should now be running on the Arduino. The sketch we uploaded does not do anything. However, it is a good way of verifying that our setup is correct. In *Chapter 3, Central Air and Heating Thermostat*, we will dive into Arduino in more detail.

Next, let's quickly look at the Arduino to Raspberry Pi connection bridge shield.

Using the Arduino to Raspberry Pi connection bridge

The Arduino to Raspberry Pi connection bridge hardware provides a convenient method to connect our Raspberry Pi to some of the Arduino shields that are available. Thus, we can reuse hardware between our two devices.

The shield's **I/O (Input/Output)** options include:

- A socket for wireless modules
- RX/TX pins
- i2C pins (SDA and SCL)
- SPI pins (SCK, MISO, MOSI, and CS), which can also be used as GPIO.
- An 8-channel analog to digital converter.
- Switch to enable external power supply

You might remember seeing these in the diagram in the previous chapter.

For more information on their functionality, you can go to the Cooking Hacks website, at http://www.cooking-hacks.com/documentation/tutorials/raspberry-pi-to-arduino-shields-connection-bridge.

In *Chapter 6, Curtain Automation – Open and Close the Curtains Based on the Ambient Light,* we will download the arduPi library in the Raspberry Pi. The arduPi library provides us with a software library that allows us to write Arduino-style C++ code in the Raspberry Pi that looks similar to Arduino sketches. This code can then control the bridge shield I/O pins and any Arduino shields or electronics connected to them.

There are several releases of the library available, depending on which model of the Raspberry Pi you purchased. You may be interested in checking out which version you have and making a note of this now.

Cooking Hacks provides a guide about this connection bridge, at http://www.cooking-hacks.com/documentation/tutorials/raspberry-pi-to-arduino-shields-connection-bridge#step3.

This overview covers the last of our hardware components. We are now ready and can start using these devices. First, let's quickly recap what we covered.

Summary

In this chapter, we looked at what an SD card is, setting it up to use it with the Raspberry Pi, installing an operating system, and loading our Raspberry Pi for the first time. We also downloaded the Arduino IDE and uploaded a test sketch to ensure that our setup was correct. In future chapters, we will cover the IDE in depth. Finally, we took a brief look at the Arduino to Raspberry Pi connection bridge in preparation for future projects and touched upon the arduPi library.

Now that we have our hardware in place, we can take a look at our first project—building a central air and heating thermostat. In this project, which will be in the next chapter, we will be using an Arduino Uno along with a relay and thermistor to control a central heating or cooling device such as a boiler, furnace, or central air conditioning system.

3
Central Air and Heating Thermostat

In this chapter, you will learn how to build a thermostat device using an Arduino. You will also learn how to use the temperature data to switch relays on and off. **Relays** are the main components that you can use for interaction between your Arduino and high-voltage electronic devices. The thermostat will also provide a web interface so that you can connect to it and check out the temperature.

Our example project will involve switching an electric fan on when the temperature rises above a set point of 25 degrees Celsius, and then switching it off when the temperature drops. We can use an ice cube and a hair dryer, or a similar device to stimulate the thermistor.

The code that controls the Arduino will also be ready to return data in a format that will be easy to insert into a database. We will create this database in *Chapter 4, Temperature Storage – Setting Up a Database to Store Your Results*.

Upon completion of the thermostat, you will have a device that you can use in your home to control a variety of devices beyond the fan example.

To build the thermostat you will need:

- An Arduino Uno microcontroller and wall power unit
- A Pololu Basic SPDT relay carrier
- An Ethernet shield such as the Seeed Ethernet shield
- An AM2302 thermistor device
- A small mains-powered electric desktop fan

- Some wire cutters and strippers
- A way of stimulating the thermistor for both low and high temperatures, for example, some ice and a hair dryer

Safety first

In this chapter, we will be using a device plugged into the mains electricity (usually AC)—a fan. We will also be cutting the cable that connects the fan to the plug socket. This cable will be run through our relay circuit.

It is important to remind you at this point that working with mains electricity is dangerous. You should attempt the fan portion of this project and hooking it up to your **Heating, Ventilation and Air Conditioning (HVAC)** system only if you feel 100 percent confident in your ability to safely attach the thermostat device to the mains.

It is also important that you select the correct relays for your electrical system. For example, attempting to use a 130V AC relay on a 240V AC electrical system can result in melting your device or something worse.

Depending on your country of residence, the mains voltage can be between 110V and 240V. Before attempting this project, we recommend reading up on your electric system.

 Wikipedia provides an overview of mains electricity that you can use as a starting point, at http://en.wikipedia.org/wiki/Mains_ electricity.

Feel free to build the thermostat device and stop when it comes to the final steps of wiring it up if you don't feel comfortable with your ability. You can always revisit this project at a later date if you wish.

With that said, let's explore what a thermostat does.

Introducing the thermostat

A **thermostat** is a control device that is used to manipulate other devices based on a temperature setting. This temperature setting is known as the **setpoint**. When the temperature changes in relation to the setpoint, a device can be switched on or off.

For example, let's imagine a system where a simple thermostat is set to switch an electric heater on when the temperature drops below 25 degrees Celsius.

Within our thermostat, we have a temperature-sensing device such as a thermistor that returns a temperature reading every few seconds. When the thermistor reads a temperature below the setpoint (25 degrees Celsius), the thermostat will switch a relay on, completing the circuit between the wall plug and our electric heater and providing it with power. Thus, we can see that a simple electronic thermostat can be used to switch on a variety of devices.

Warren S. Johnson, a college professor in Wisconsin, is credited with inventing the electric room thermostat in the 1880s. Johnson was known throughout his lifetime as a prolific inventor who worked in a variety of fields, including electricity. These electric room thermostats became a common feature in homes across the course of the twentieth century as larger parts of the world were hooked up the electricity grid.

Now, with open hardware electronic tools such as the Arduino available, we can build custom thermostats for a variety of home projects. They can be used to control baseboard heaters, heat lamps, and air conditioner units. They can also be used for the following:

- Fish tank heaters
- Indoor gardens
- Electric heaters
- Fans

Now that we have explored the uses of thermostats, let's take a look at our project.

Setting up our hardware

In the following examples, we will list the pins to which you need to connect your hardware. However, we recommend that when you purchase any device such as the Ethernet shield, you check whether certain pins are available or not. Due to the sheer range of hardware available, it is not possible to list every potential hardware combination. Therefore, if the pin in the example is not free, you can update the circuit and source code to use a different pin.

When building the example, we also recommend using a breadboard. This will allow you to experiment with building your circuit without having to solder any components.

Our first task will be to set up our thermostat device so that it has Ethernet access.

Adding the Ethernet shield

The Arduino Uno does not contain an Ethernet port. Therefore, you will need a way for your thermostat to be accessible on your home network.

One simple solution is to purchase an Ethernet shield and connect it to your microcontroller.

 There are several shields in the market, including the Arduino Ethernet shield (`http://arduino.cc/en/Main/ArduinoEthernetShield`) and Seeed Ethernet shield (`http://www.seeedstudio.com/wiki/Ethernet_Shield_V1.0`).

These shields are plugged into the GPIO pins on the Arduino. If you purchase one of these shields, then we would also recommend buying some extra GPIO headers. These are plugged into the existing headers attached to the Ethernet shield. Their purpose is to provide some extra clearance above the Ethernet port on the board so that you can connect other shields in future if you decide to purchase them.

Take a board of your choice and attach it to the Arduino Uno. When you plug the USB cable into your microcontroller and into your computer, the lights on both the Uno and Ethernet shield should light up. Later in this chapter, we will write code that allows our thermostat to use the shield.

Now our device has a medium to send and receive data over a LAN. Let's take a look at setting up our thermostat relays.

Relays

A **relay** is a type of switch controlled by an electromagnet. It allows us to use a small amount of power to control a much larger amount, for example, using a 9V power supply to switch 220V wall power. Relays are rated to work with different voltages and currents.

A relay has three contact points: **Normally Open**, **Common Connection**, and **Normally Closed**. Two of these points will be wired up to our fan. In the context of an Arduino project, the relay will also have a pin for ground, 5V power and a data pin that is used to switch the relay on and off.

A popular choice for a relay is the Pololu Basic SPDT Relay Carrier.

 This can be purchased from `http://www.pololu.com/category/135/relay-modules`.

This relay has featured in some other Packt Publishing books on the Arduino, so it is a good investment.

Once you have the relay, you need to wire it up to the microcontroller. Connect a wire from the relay to digital pin 5 on the Arduino, another wire to the GRD pin, and the final wire to the 5V pin.

When working with the projects in this book, you will be switching between using the Arduino and Raspberry Pi. Therefore, it is worth mentioning that the GPIO pins on the Raspberry Pi use 3.3V, but the Arduino Uno has both 5V and 3.3V pins. So you should be careful when you mix and match GPIOs.

This completes the relay setup. In order to control relays though, we need some data to trigger switching them between on and off. Our thermistor device handles the task of collecting this data.

Connecting the thermistor

A **thermistor** is an electronic component that, when included in a circuit, can be used to measure temperature. The device is a type of resistor that has the property whereby its resistance varies as the temperature changes. It can be found in a variety of devices, including thermostats and electronic thermometers.

There are two categories of thermistors available: **Negative Thermistor Coefficient (NTC)** and **Positive Thermistor Coefficient (PTC)**. The difference between them is that as the temperature increases, the resistance decreases in the case of an NTC, and on the other hand, it increases in the case of a PTC.

We are going to use a prebuilt digital device with the model number AM2303.

This can be purchased at `https://www.adafruit.com/products/393`.

This device reads both temperature and humidity. It also comes with a software library that you can use in your Arduino sketches. One of the benefits of this library is that many functions that precompute values, such as temperature in Celsius, are available and thus don't require you to write a lot of code.

Take your AM203 and connect it to the GRD pin, 5V pin and digital pin 4.
The following diagram shows how it should be set up:

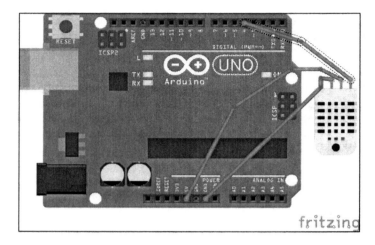

You are now ready to move on to creating the software to test for
temperature readings.

Setting up our software

We now need to write an application in the Arduino IDE to control our new
thermostat device. Our software will contain the following:

- The code responsible for collecting the temperature data
- Methods to switch relays on and off based on this data
- Code to handle accepting incoming HTTP requests so that we can view
  our thermostat's current temperature reading and change the setpoint
- A method to send our temperature readings to the Raspberry Pi

The next step is to hook up our Arduino thermostat with the USB port of the device
we installed the IDE on.

You may need to temporarily disconnect your relay from the
Arduino. This will prevent your thermostat device from drawing
too much power from your computer's USB port, which may
result in the port being disabled.

We now need to download the DHT library that interacts with our AM2303.

 This can be found on GitHub, at `https://github.com/adafruit/DHT-sensor-library`.

1. Click on the **Download ZIP** link and unzip the file to a location on your hard drive.
2. Next, we need to install the library to make it accessible from our sketch:
    1. Open the Arduino IDE.
    2. Navigate to **Sketch | Import Library**.
    3. Next, click on **Add library**.
    4. Choose the folder on your hard drive.
    5. You can now use the library.

With the library installed, we can include it in our sketch and access a number of useful functions. Let's now start creating our software.

Thermostat software

We can start adding some code to the Arduino to control our thermostat. Open a new sketch in the Arduino IDE and perform the following steps:

1. Inside the sketch, we are going to start by adding the code to include the libraries we need to use. At the top of the sketch, add the following code:

```
#include "DHT.h" // Include this if using the AM2302
#include <SPI.h>
#include <Ethernet.h>
```

2. Next, we will declare some variables to be used by our application. These will be responsible for defining:
    ° The pin the AM2303 thermistor is located on
    ° The relay pin
    ° The IP address we want our Arduino to use, which should be unique
    ° The Mac address of the Arduino, which should also be unique
    ° The name of the room the thermostat is located in
    ° The variables responsible for Ethernet communication

3. The IP address will depend on your own home network. Check out your wireless router to see what range of IP addresses is available. Select an address that isn't in use and update the IPAddress variable as follows:

```
#define DHTPIN 4 // The digital pin to read from
#define DHTTYPE DHT22 // DHT 22 (AM2302)

unsigned char relay = 5; //The relay pins
String room = "library";
byte mac[] = { 0xDE, 0xAD, 0xBE, 0xEF, 0xFE, 0xED };
IPAddress ip(192,168,3,5);
DHT dht(DHTPIN, DHTTYPE);
EthernetServer server(80);
EthernetClient client;
```

4. We can now include the setup() function. This is responsible for initializing some variables with their default values, and setting the pin to which our relay is connected to output mode:

```
void setup() {
  Serial.begin(9600);
  Ethernet.begin(mac, ip);
  server.begin();
  dht.begin();
  pinMode(relay, OUTPUT);
}
```

5. The next block of code we will add is the loop() function. This contains the main body of our program to be executed. Here, we will assign a value to the setpoint and grab our temperature readings:

```
void loop() {
  int setpoint = 25;
  float h = dht.readHumidity();
  float t = dht.readTemperature();
```

6. Following this, we check whether the temperature is above or below the setpoint and switch the relay on or off as needed. Paste this code below the variables you just added:

```
if(t <setpoint) {
  digitalWrite(relay,HIGH);
} else {
  digitalWrite(relay,LOW);
}
```

7. Next, we need to handle the HTTP requests to the thermostat. We start by collecting all of the incoming data. The following code also goes inside the `loop()` function:

```
client = server.available();
if (client) {
  // an http request ends with a blank line
  booleancurrentLineIsBlank = true;
  String result;
  while (client.connected()) {
    if (client.available()) {
      char c = client.read();
      result= result + c;
    }
```

8. With the incoming request stored in the result variable, we can examine the HTTP header to know whether we are requesting an HTML page or a JSON object. You'll learn more about **JavaScript Object Notation (JSON)** shortly. If we request an HTML page, this is displayed in the browser. Next, add the following code to your sketch:

```
if(result.indexOf("text/html") > -1) {
  client.println("HTTP/1.1 200 OK");
  client.println("Content-Type: text/html");
  client.println();
  if (isnan(h) || isnan(t)) {
    client.println("Failed to read from DHT sensor!");
    return;
  }
  client.print("<b>Thermostat</b> set to: ");
  client.print(setpoint);
  client.print("degrees C <br />Humidity: ");
  client.print(h);
  client.print(" %\t");
  client.print("<br />Temperature: ");
  client.print(t);
  client.println(" degrees C ");
  break;
}
```

The following code handles a request for the data to be returned in JSON format. Our Raspberry Pi will make HTTP requests to the Arduino, and then process the data returned to it. At the bottom of this last block of code is a statement adding a short delay to allow the Arduino to process the request and close the client connection.

9. Paste this final section of code in your sketch:

```
if( result.indexOf("application/json") > -1 ) {
client.println("HTTP/1.1 200 OK");
client.println("Content-Type: application/json;charset=utf-8");
client.println("Server: Arduino");
client.println("Connnection: close");
client.println();
client.print("{\"thermostat\":[{\"location\":\"");
client.print(room);
client.print("\"},");
client.print("{\"temperature\":\"");
client.print(t);
client.print("\"},");
client.print("{\"humidity\":\"");
client.print(h);
client.print("\"},");
client.print("{\"setpoint\":\"");
client.print(setpoint);
client.print("\"}");
client.print("]}");
client.println();
break;
        }
    }
delay(1);
client.stop();
    }
}
```

10. This completes our program. We can now save it and run the Verify process. Click on the small check mark in a circle located in the top-left corner of the sketch. If you have added all of the code correctly, you should see **Binary sketch size: 16,962 bytes (of a 32,256 byte maximum)**.

> **Downloading the example code**
>
> You can download the example code files from your account at http://www.packtpub.com for all the Packt Publishing books you have purchased. If you purchased this book elsewhere, you can visit http://www.packtpub.com/support and register to have the files e-mailed directly to you.

Now that our code is verified and saved, we can look at uploading it to the Arduino, attaching the fan, and testing our thermostat.

Testing our thermostat and fan

We have our hardware set up and the code ready. Now we can test the thermostat and see it in action with a device connected to the mains electricity. We will first attach a fan and then run the sketch to switch it on and off.

Attaching the fan

Ensure that your Arduino is powered down and that the fan is not plugged into the wall. Using a wire stripper and cutters, cut one side of the cable that connects the plug to the fan body. Take the end of the cable attached to the plug, and attach it to the NO point on the relay. Use a screwdriver to ensure that it is fastened correctly. Now, take the other portion of the cut cable that is attached to the fan body, and attach this to the COM point. Once again, use a screwdriver to ensure that it is fastened securely to the relay. Your connection should look as follows:

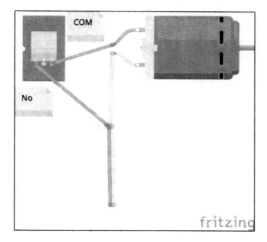

You can now reattach your Arduino to the computer via its USB cable. However, do not plug the fan into the wall yet.

Starting your thermostat application

With the fan connected to our relay, we can upload our sketch and test it:

1. From the Arudino IDE, select the upload icon. Once the code has been uploaded, disconnect your Arduino board.

2. Next, connect an Ethernet cable to your Arduino. Following this, plug the Arduino into the wall to get mains power.

3. Finally, connect the fan to the wall outlet.

4. You should hear the clicking sound of the relay as it switches on or off depending on the room temperature. When the relay switch is on (or off), the fan will follow suit.

5. Using a separate laptop if you have it, or from your Raspberry Pi, access the IP address you specified in the application via a web browser, for example, `http://192.168.3.5/`.

6. You should see something similar to this:

```
Thermostat set to: 25degrees C
Humidity: 35.70 %
Temperature: 14.90 degrees C
```

You can now stimulate the thermistor using an ice cube and hair dryer, to switch the relay on and off, and the fan will follow suit. If you refresh your connection to the IP address, you should see the change in the temperature output on the screen. You can use the *F5* key to do this. Besides returning the HTML document, our Arduino sketch also returns JSON data, which we will use in *Chapter 4, Temperature Storage – Setting Up a Database to Store Your Results*.

Let's now test the JSON response.

Testing the JSON response

A format useful in transferring data between applications is **JavaScript Object Notation (JSON)**.

> You can read more about this on the official JSON website, at `http://www.json.org/`.

The purpose of us generating data in JSON format is to allow the Raspberry Pi control device we are building to query the thermostat periodically and collect the data being generated. We can verify that we are getting JSON data back from the sketch by making an HTTP request using the `application/json` header.

Load a web browser such as Google Chrome or FireFox. We are going to make an XML HTTP request directly from the browser to our thermostat.

> This type of request is commonly known as an **Asynchronous JavaScript and XML (AJAX)** request. It can be used to refresh data on a page without having to actually reload it.

In your web browser, locate and open the developer tools.

 The following link lists the location and shortcut keys in major browsers:
`http://webmasters.stackexchange.com/questions/8525/how-to-open-the-javascript-console-in-different-browsers`

In the JavaScript console portion of the developer tools, type the following JavaScript code:

```
var xmlhttp;
xmlhttp=new XMLHttpRequest();
xmlhttp.open("POST","192.168.3.5",true);
xmlhttp.setRequestHeader("Content-type","application/json");
xmlhttp.onreadystatechange = function() {//Call a function when the
state changes.
    if(xmlhttp.readyState == 4 &&xmlhttp.status == 200) {
        console.log(xmlhttp);
    }
};
xmlhttp.send()
```

Press the *return* key or run option to execute the code.

This will fire an HTTP request, and you should see a JSON object return:

```
"{"thermostat":
    [
    {"location":"library"},
    {"temperature":"14.90"},
    {"humidity":"29.90"},
    {"setpoint":"25"}
    ]
}"
```

This confirms that our application can return data to the Raspberry Pi. We have tested our software and hardware and seen that they are working. There are many ways to extend the thermostat's feature set; the next section explores some of these.

Next steps

Congratulations! You have finished building a web-based thermostat and creating software to control it.

Now that we have the basics in place, we can add extra features and connect the device to our home heating system, fish tank, or something similar.

The following projects are optional. With the thermostat device you have built, you can continue to follow the examples in the coming chapters, skipping the following section if you wish.

You can always revisit these projects at a later date.

Attaching the device to your heating system or a similar appliance

Your next step will be to attach the thermostat to another electrical system you wish to control, for example, a heating system or fish tank. Some thermostats handle multiple systems such as heating and cooling, and if you wish to replicate this functionality, you will need to add more relays to your device and expand the sketch code to support switching multiple relays on and off. The thermostat we built works with a two-wire system.

You can read more on this at http://www.electrical-online. com/thermostat-wiring-explained/.

Start by powering the Arduino down and disconnecting the fan from the relay. Once this is done you can complete the following steps:

Remember that working with mains electricity is dangerous. This section is purely for the purpose of information. Many off-the-shelf products are not safety rated for use with systems such as furnaces. Always check out the documentation that accompanies your hardware to know whether it can be used safely for such a system. If you do not have the skill to safely attach the thermostat to your heating system, consider consulting a certified electrician.

1. Next, you will need to locate the existing thermostat on the device you wish to replace.

2. With the power switched off at the fuse box, you can now remove the existing thermostat. Once it is disassembled, make a note of the wiring and how it was attached to the old equipment. If you wish to reattach your existing thermostat after you finish experimenting, this note will come in handy.

3. You should see a white wire and a red wire. These will be connected to the relay, and when the relay closes, it completes the circuit that turns your system on.

You are advised not to attempt this process with baseboard heating units, as these tend to have higher control voltages.

4. Attach the wires to your relay as you did with the fan. You can use the guide at the link provided previously for help.
5. Once the thermostat is wired up, you can turn on the power again from the fuse box.
6. Power up your Arduino and hook it up with your home network. If you check out the IP address of your device in the browser, you should see the current room temperature.

The Arduino thermostat should also switch whichever heating system you have plugged it into on and off as needed, based on the setpoint value.

Adding a potentiometer

A potentiometer is added so that you can change the temperature on the device manually. A simple potentiometer can be connected to one of your analog pins, for example, analog 2. Then it is also connected to the GRD and 5V pins. When the potentiometer is twisted, its resistance is changed.

Using the value returned from the analog pin, you can update your setpoint value.

The Arduino website provides a simple introduction to understanding potentiometers, at http://www.arduino.cc/en/tutorial/potentiometer.

Let's assume that you have set initialSetPoint as a constant at the top of your sketch. The following code provides an example of how you could update the setpoint:

```
int potentiometer = 2;
int setpoint;

void setup() {
}
```

```
void loop() {
  setpoint= (initialSetPoint - analogRead(potentiometer));
}
```

You may need to adjust the value being returned from the `analogRead()` function to have it decrement or increment `setpoint` by a suitable amount. For example, if you are not running equipment such as a furnace, you may want to scale down the value returned, as `analogRead` returns a value between 0 and 1023.

To do this, you can use the map function:

```
setpoint = initialSetPoint - map(analogRead(potentiometer), 0, 1023,
10, 40)
```

What if we wish to see the value being changed by the potentiometer? This is where a screen becomes useful.

Adding an LCD screen

An LCD screen provides a good way of displaying the temperature in real time. There are many devices available, from simple LCD screens to more complex devices with buttons and micro SD card ports. Before purchasing a screen, download the schematics and the source library for the board. This will give you an idea if you have the free digital pins available to implement it.

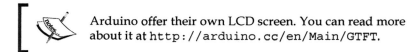

Arduino offer their own LCD screen. You can read more about it at `http://arduino.cc/en/Main/GTFT`.

Once you have hooked up the screen, you will need to update your Arduino sketch.

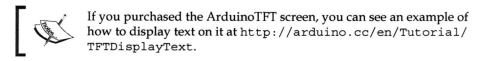

If you purchased the ArduinoTFT screen, you can see an example of how to display text on it at `http://arduino.cc/en/Tutorial/TFTDisplayText`.

It is easy to modify the block of code that returns the temperature to also output this data to the LCD screen. This completes our list of future enhancements. Let's now summarize the chapter.

Summary

In this chapter, we built a thermostat device. We looked at thermistors, and you learned how to set up an Ethernet connection. To control our thermostat, we wrote an Arduino sketch, uploaded it to the microcontroller, and then tested it with a fan plugged into the mains electricity.

Finally, we reviewed some steps to expand the device so that it can accommodate an LCD screen and potentiometer to change the observed temperature.

Next, we will look at building a database to store the values returned from our thermostat. This will be done in our first project using the Raspberry Pi.

4
Temperature Storage – Setting Up a Database to Store Your Results

In the next few chapters, the Raspberry Pi will act as a central control device to read data from our Arduino devices, control DC motors, and send e-mails. In this chapter, we will cover setting up a database on the Raspberry Pi using **SQLite**.

This SQL database will be a place to store the results from the temperature readings that we captured in the previous chapter. We will also look at **HyperText Structured Query Language (HTSQL)**, a language that allows us to query our database via HTTP requests.

Along with these technologies, we will set up a Python script that grabs the temperature reading from the Arduino and writes it to the database. This script will be run periodically via a cron job.

For this chapter, you will need the following:

- The Raspberry Pi you set up
- Optionally, a monitor, keyboard, and mouse plugged into your Raspberry Pi if you don't plan to connect over SSH
- The Arduino thermostat you built in the previous chapter

Let's get started. Our first step will be to SSH into our Raspberry Pi, install SQLite 3.x, and set up our control database.

SSH

In the first chapter, we verified that SSH was up and running on Raspbian. In order to connect to the SSH service that we started, you will need the Raspberry Pi's IP address.

There are several ways of getting the IP address assigned to your Raspberry Pi, one of which is to check out the DHCP table on your home modem or router. However, an easier method is to check it out on the Raspberry Pi itself.

 There are several types of IP address, including public and private. We will be using a private IP address range on our home network.

To do this, power up your Raspberry Pi and load LXTerminal again. Then type the following command:

```
ipaddr show eth0
```

 You can find your IP address after `Inet`, like this:
`Inet 192.168.3.122/24 brd 192.168.3.255 scope global eth0`
You need the portion before /. It reads `192.168.3.122`.

 An IP address is a way of assigning a unique identifier to a computer or device on a local network or the Internet. The most common form of IP addresses at the moment is IPv6, which takes a format similar to `2001:0ab1:25b9:0047:0000:8a2e:0110:7444`.

Once you have the IP address for your Raspberry Pi, you can try connecting to it from another machine. Mac and Linux users can use the terminal that comes shipped with their operating system.

 Windows users can download a terminal-executable file called PuTTY from `http://www.chiark.greenend.org.uk/~sgtatham/putty/download.html`.

PuTTY provides Windows users with a terminal-style window that they can use to connect to Linux machines.

Windows users should follow these steps to set up PuTTY on their Windows machine:

1. Double-click on the `putty.exe` file to load the PuTTY configuration screen.

2. In the **Host Name** (or **IP address**) text entry field, add the IP address of your Raspberry Pi.

3. Enter 22 in the **Port** field, and under **Connection type**, select **SSH**.

4. Finally, click on **Open**.

5. You may see a pop-up box with the title, **PuTTY Security Alert**, and a message explaining that the server's host key is not cached in the registry Select the **Yes** button.

6. In the terminal window, you will now see the following message:

   `Login as:`

   Enter your Raspberry Pi username, that is, `pi`.

7. You will now see another message asking for the password, like this:

   `pi@192.168.3.122's password:`

8. Enter the password and press the *Enter* key.

[The default password is `raspberry`.]

You will now be logged in to the Raspberry Pi. Congratulations! You can now connect to your Raspberry Pi from your Windows machine, and set up your database using SQLite3.

If you are a Mac or Linux user, follow these steps:

Once you have your Terminal application ready, you can connect to your Raspberry Pi via SSH using the following command:

`ssh pi@192.168.3.122`

1. You will be asked to enter your password and may see a message suggesting that the authenticity of the host can't be established, like this:

   `The authenticity of host '192.168.3.122 (192.168.3.122)' can't be established.`

   `RSA key fingerprint is f6:4a:38:4a:8b:c6:04:a9:bc:51:c3:af:fe:cb:78:e6.`

   `Are you sure you want to continue connecting (yes/no)?`

2. Type `yes` in the command line and press the *Enter* key.

3. You will then see the following message:

    ```
    Warning: Permanently added '192.168.3.122' (RSA) to the list of known
      hosts.
    ```

4. Once you have completed this and entered your password, you should see the command line for your Raspberry Pi.

You have now successfully logged in to your Raspberry Pi via SSH. Let's now set up SQLite.

SQLite

SQLite 3.x is the latest version of the SQLite series of database technologies. Written in the C programming language, SQLite is a relational database management system that has continued to support more SQL standards as it progressed through several versions.

This means that many of the features you may be familiar with within SQL are available to use when creating a SQLite database.

SQLite has many uses, which include creating databases to embed in applications such as web browsers, or creating lightweight databases for embedded systems running on hardware such as the Raspberry Pi. It is also practical for small projects that do not require a very complex and maintenance-heavy RDMS, such as Oracle or MS SQL, and for those looking for a free and easy solution to store data.

 You can read more about the technology and the latest features it supports at `http://www.sqlite.org/`.

Installing SQLite Version 3.x

We will now walk through the process of installing SQLite on our Raspberry Pi. You can either log in to your Raspberry Pi via SSH or connect over the desktop and open LXTerminal. Once logged in, run `apt-get` to install SQLite3.

In the command line, type this:

```
sudo apt-get install sqlite3
```

If you run `sudo apt-get install sqlite`, it will only install SQLite 2.x. Version 2.x does not support some of the commands we will be using, such as `ALTER TABLE`. So make sure you use `sqlite3` when using `apt-get`.

The terminal will show you the feedback as it installs SQLite. Once the installation is completed, navigate to your home directory (if you are not there already) and create a new directory, within which we will work. Type the following commands in your terminal window:

```
cd ~
mkdir database
cd database
```

This database directory will be used to store our `control` database to test and demonstrate how to use SQLite.

Creating a database

To load SQLite, simply type `sqlite3` followed by the database name and the `.db` extension. If the database does not exist, `sqlite3` will create it for you, for example, `mydatabase.db`.

For our project, we will name the database `control`. This database will also be used in other projects and will act as the main storage mechanism for our Raspberry Pi control device.

In the command line, type the following:

```
sqlite3 control.db
```

You will now be dropped into the SQLite3 shell. From the SQLite shell, we can type commands that will create tables in the database and assign to them columns within which we will store data. Before creating anything in our database, we should consider which tables and columns we are going to need.

For this project, we only need a simple data structure. Two tables should be enough to record the data we want to store. One table will be responsible for storing the temperature data, and the other for recording the details of the room the Arduino is located in.

Let's look at the `Temperature` table first.

A table to record our temperature

The Temperature table will be responsible for storing the data written back from the Arduino shield. We will need the following columns in this table:

- ID: This will be the unique ID for each temperature reading written to the database. With each new value added, it should increment automatically, and should also be the primary key for our table.

- RoomID: This will serve the purpose of linking the temperature reading to a table containing information about the room it was taken from via a foreign key; for example, in our project, we will store the name of the room there.

- TemperatureC: This column will be used to store our temperature reading in degrees Celsius. This value will have been calculated by the Arduino and grabbed in JSON format for our Python script to insert into the database.

- Datetime: We will calculate a timestamp for each reading when inserting data into the table. This can be useful when querying the database and trying to find out some special information, for example, the time periods for which a given room is coldest.

A table to record our rooms

The second table that we will create will store the name of the room in it. This table can be expanded later to include extra details about the room. To start with it, however, we will only need two columns:

- ID: This will be a unique ID for the room. It will be incremented with every room added. When we add data to the Temperature table, we will insert this room ID. This way, if we decide to rename the room, we only have to update a single value in one table, rather than replace multiple instances, which would be the case if we had recorded the name of the room next to each temperature reading in the Temperature table.

- RoomName: The second column is used to store the name of room. Here, we can store a value such as Bathroom or Kitchen.

Writing SQL queries

With the designs of our two tables planned, we can create them using SQL:

1. From the SQLite3 shell, enter the following SQL command:

```
CREATE TABLE RoomDetails (ID INTEGER PRIMARY KEY AUTOINCREMENT,
Room VARCHAR(25));
```

2. This command creates a new table called `RoomDetails` and adds an ID column that takes integer values. This column is the primary key of the table, and with each new value that is added, the ID is incremented by 1. Next, we will create the `Temperature` table. Type the following SQL command in the SQLite3 shell:

```
CREATE TABLE Temperature (ID INTEGER PRIMARY KEY AUTOINCREMENT,
RoomID INTEGER, FOREIGN KEY(RoomID) REFERENCES RoomDetails(ID));
```

The preceding command has created our second table, called `Temperature`. This table will be used to store each of our temperature readings. The SQL command has created two columns, the first being the ID, which is an integer and is incremented automatically. The second column created will be used to store the room IDs. This column references `RoomDetails` and creates a foreign key link to it. Now that we have the `Temperature` table, we can add two more columns to it— `TemperatureC` and `Datetime`.

3. For this task, we can use the `ALTER TABLE` SQL command in order to add a new column to an existing database. From within the SQLite3 shell, enter this SQL command:

```
ALTER TABLE Temperature ADD COLUMN TemperatureC FLOAT(8);
```

We have now updated our `Temperature` table and added the column to store the temperature readings from the sensor on the Arduino Uno. This column accepts numeric float values that are eight characters long, which means we can store decimal numbers such as 52.3, 48.4, and so on.

4. Finally, let's add the date stamp column to our database so that we can check when our temperature readings were stored. Using the shell, execute the following command:

```
ALTER TABLE Temperature ADD COLUMN Datetime DATETIME;
```

We have now added our final `Datetime` column to the table. This column takes a date-formatted value in the `YYYY-MM-DD HH:MM:SS` format.

With the two tables in place, let's add a room to the `RoomDetails` table. This could be the room that you have your Arduino thermostat running in.

In the previous chapter, we added the `Library` placeholder to the Arduino code. We will go back and change this to the code of the room you have decided to use.

In the following example, we will use `Library` as the value:

1. From within the SQLite3 shell, execute the following command:

   ```
   INSERT INTO RoomDetails (Room) VALUES ('Library');
   ```

2. Now you can check whether your room is present using this command:

   ```
   SELECT * FROM RoomDetails;
   ```

   This command selects all the values from the `RoomDetails` table and displays them. If you added `Library` as your room, you should see this:

   ```
   1|Library
   ```

   Now we have a room in our database with an ID of `1`, which we can use when writing data back from the Arduino application.

3. You can now exit the database. From the shell, type the following command to exit SQLite3:

   ```
   .quit
   ```

4. You next step is to update the Arduino code to use the ID that was just displayed. Open the sketch from *Chapter 3, Central Air and Heating Thermostat*, and modify the following lines:

   ```
   client.print("{\"thermostat\":[{\"location\":\"");
   client.print(room);
   ```

5. Replace `room` with the value of `1`, or create a new variable, assign `1` to it, and replace `room` with the new variable reference.

6. Save your Arduino code, upload it to your Arduino, save, and exit.

Next, we are going to create a Python application that grabs data from the Arduino and writes it to the database.

Creating a Python application to write to our database

The following Python application is going to connect to our Arduino through an HTTP request, and process the JSON data in the response. This will be achieved by setting the HTTP header in our request to the following:

```
'application/json;charset=utf-8'
```

As you may remember, our Arduino application is specifically set up to look for incoming requests of this format.

1. Start by creating a new, empty file in the database folder, called `request.py`:

2. With your new file open, add the following code to it:

```
#!/usr/bin/env python
import sqlite3
import urllib2
import json
```

This block of code is responsible for importing libraries that we can use to:

- ° Connect to a SQLite database
- ° Craft an HTTP request
- ° Convert JSON data into a Python dictionary

3. After adding the import statements, we can start writing our `main()` function. Add the following code below the import statements:

```
def main():
    req = urllib2.Request('http://192.168.3.5/')
    req.add_header('Content-Type', 'application/
json;charset=utf-8')
    r = urllib2.urlopen(req)
    result = json.load(r)
```

Here, we create an HTTP request to the Arduino. You will need to change the IP address to that of your microcontroller. As you can see, we set the HTTP header to `application/json:charset=utf-8` so that the Arduino returns the temperature data in JSON.

4. We then make the HTTP request. We store the data in a variable called `result` using a function called `load()` from the `json` library. Following this, we need extract the values we want to store in the database.

5. Next, add the following block of code. Remember to indent it using four spaces:

```
room = result['thermostat'][0]['location']
temperature = result['thermostat'][1]['temperature']
my_query = 'INSERT INTO Temperature(RoomID,TemperatureC,Datetime)
\
VALUES(%s,%s,CURRENT_TIMESTAMP);' % (Room,Temperature)
```

Here we have created `room` and `temperature` variables from the values stored in the `results` variable.

6. Next, we create a small SQL query that inserts these two variables into the temperature table, along with a timestamp. We need to execute this query, so we add this code:

```
try:
    connection =  sqlite3.connect('/home/pi/database/control.
db',isolation_level=None)
    cursor = connection.cursor()
    cursor.execute(my_query)
    query_results = cursor.fetchone()
    my_response = 'Inserted %s for room %s' % (temperature, room)
except sqlite3.Error, e:
    my_response = "There is an error %s:" % (e)
finally:
    print my_response
    connection.close()
```

These statements are responsible for connecting to the database and executing our query. They rely on the functionality provided by the `sqlite3` library. You may notice this code is wrapped in blocks called `try`, `except`, and `finally`.

The way this works is we attempt to execute the code in the `try` block. If this fails, then the `except` block is executed. Finally, as the name suggests, the `finally` block is executed regardless of whether there was an error or we ran our query successfully.

Let's look at the `try` block first.

You will need to update the path in the `connect()` function to point to the SQLite database you created earlier in this chapter. This creates the connection to our database so that we can run queries. Following this, we execute our query and assign a confirmation message that the temperature was inserted into the `my_response` variable.

If this process fails, then the `except` block is run. It captures the error thrown by SQLite and assigns it to the `my_response` variable, with some text wrapped around it. After either the `try` or `except` block has completed, our `finally` block runs.

Here, we output the message that we had stored in the `my_response` variable and close our connection to the database. This completes the main portion of our code. We will wrap up the script with the following block of code. This executes the `main()` function when the script is called:

```
if __name__ == "__main__":
    main()
```

Save the code and go back to the shell.

Checking the results

With our script complete, it is now time to run it and see what results we get. We can run the Python script from the Raspberry Pi command line in the following way:

```
python request.py
```

You should see this output:

```
Inserted 13.1 for room 1
```

Having run the script to check your database, start by opening the SQLite shell:

```
sqlite3 control.db
```

Next, run the following query:

```
SELECT * from Temperature;
```

You will see something like this:

```
1|1|13.1|2014-01-24 10:17:06
```

This confirms that our script is running correctly. Each time you run the application, you should see a new entry in your database. This finishes our script that writes the temperature and room to the database. We could also expand this to include the humidity value that is returned.

As useful as this script is, it is not convenient to run it manually. We can automate this process using a cron job.

Adding a cron job

A cron job is a method that allows the operating system to periodically run scripts, tasks, and other programs without the user requiring to log in and run them themselves. Cron is built into the Raspbian operating system, so we have no extra software to install. We simply have to edit the cron table (crontab) and add a timestamp and path to the script we want to run:

1. We can see which cron jobs are currently running on our Raspberry Pi by typing this:

    ```
    crontab -l
    ```

    You may notice that there are no jobs in the list.

2. To edit the file, we use the -e flag:

    ```
    crontab -e
    ```

3. Once it is open, you should see a comment in the file showing the structure of a cron job:

```
# m h dom mon dow    command
```

> You can read more about the cron table format at
> http://www.adminschoice.com/crontab-quick-reference.

4. We want to take a reading once an hour. However, we can quickly test the script to ensure that the cron job is working.

   To do this, add the following code to your cron table, and remember to update the path to point to where your request.py is stored:

```
* * * * python /<path>/<to>/request.py
```

   The * symbol is a wildcard, and our script will run in very short time intervals, for example, every minute.

5. Log in to your SQLite database and run the following query:

```
SELECT * FROM Temperature;
```

   The query should return a group of results. Each time you run the query, you should start to see the list of results grow, like this:

```
1|1|13.1|2014-01-24 10:17:06
2|1|12.8|2014-01-24 21:30:02
3|1|12.8|2014-01-24 21:31:02
```

6. We can now update crontab such that it runs once an hour. Exit SQLite and re-open crontab.

7. Change the entry so that the first value is 0. Your cron job should look as follows:

```
0 * * * python /<path>/<to>/request.py
```

   Save and exit.

> You can output any errors from the script to a file
> by adding > output.log to the end of the entry in
> crontab.

Our script will now run once an hour, adding data to our SQLite database.

Now we need a method to view this data via the Web without having to log in to SQLite3 and write queries. The tool that we are going to use for this is HTSQL.

HTSQL

Hyper Text Structured Query Language (HTSQL) is a technology that allows us to write queries on the fly for our database and execute them via a URL. Developed by Clark Evans and Kirill Simonov of Prometheus Research, HTSQL is built upon the Python programming language and provides an HTTP-based query language that is translated into SQL. This allows us to write complex queries via the web browser, and allows queries to be embedded in client-side AJAX code without the need to write server-side applications.

Unlike SQL and server-side programming languages such as Java, a database with an HTSQL server running on it can be accessed via JavaScript or a web browser, such as Midori. The benefit of using this technology is that it cuts down on the amount of server-side code we have to write, and also provides us with a simpler syntax than SQL to query a database.

You might remember that we wrote the following SQL query to return the values in our Temperature table:

```
SELECT * FROM Temperature;
```

In order to execute this, we need to be connected to our database via the SQLite3 shell, or we need to write a Python application with the query in it.

To access the same data via HTSQL, we can simply use /temperature in the URL bar of our browser after the URL of our Raspberry Pi, for example, http://localhost:8080/temperature.

An HTSQL server is very simple to set up on our Raspberry Pi, so let's get started by installing the necessary packages.

Downloading HTSQL

We are now going to install HTSQL, but we will need to install Python-pip first. This is a Python-based package management system that we will be using to install HTSQL:

```
sudo apt-get install python-pip
```

A message will be displayed, informing you that the installation will take 14.5 MB of disk space. You can press Y and *Enter* to continue with the installation process. Once the installation is complete, we can use pip to install HTSQL. Type the following in the command line:

```
sudo pip install HTSQL
```

The HTSQL installation process will kick off, and once it is complete, we can check whether it was successful. In the command line, type this expression:

```
htsql-ctl version
```

You should see the terminal window of the version of HTSQL that you have installed.

However, it will be the latest version in the case of pip.

Configuring HTSQL

The next step is to configure HTSQL, point it to our database, and then set up a server to allow us to query the database via our web browser. We can test our connection to the control database we created, as follows:

```
htsql-ctl shell sqlite:path/control.db
```

This creates a shell similar to the SQLite3 shell on the database we created. In the preceding example, SQLite is the database type, and the path follows it, completed by the database filename. Once you log in to the database via the HTSQL shell, you can proceed with running a server:

1. Quit the HTSQL shell. From the command line, create an HTSQL server:

    ```
    htsql-ctl server 'sqlite:path/control.db'
    ```

    As with the preceding shell connection, the path should be replaced with the path to the database that we added to the /home/pi/database folder, or if you decide to use another directory, use that path instead.

2. Once the server has started, you will see the following message in the command line:

    ```
    Starting an HTSQL server on raspberrypi:8080 over ../database/
    control.db
    ```

    We can now check whether HTSQL is running as expected.

    Load your web browser either on the Raspberry Pi or remotely, and in the URL bar, type http://<ip of raspberry pi>:8080. You should see a message as shown in the following screenshot:

Welcome to HTSQL!

Please enter a query in the address bar.

3. You can then display the `room` table we created by typing `http://<ip of raspberry pi>:8080/roomdetails`.

    The database is now viewable via the web browser, and the data can be seen in the `Temperature` table as it gets added.

4. In order to query the data, we can use the `/roomdetails{id}` syntax. You can place column IDs from your database between the braces separated by commas, and only these columns will be returned when you execute the query:

    /roomdetails?id='1'

    Placing a question mark after the table name or the braces allows us to provide conditional statements such as showing all of the data located in all the columns where the ID is equal to 1. In the case of our database, this should return a single result, and all the column values for that result.

5. We can test whether our data has made its way through the system by querying the `control` database via HTSQL, as we did with regular SQL.

    For example, if we want to see the room, temperature, and timestamp, we can use the `http://<ip of raspberry pi>:8080/temperature{room,temperaturec,datetime}?roomid='1'` query.

You should now see an HTML table listing the room data, temperature, and timestamp.

HTSQL has extensive syntax and allows you to write complex queries to return data in a variety of formats, including JSON, XML, CSV, text, and YAML.

> You can read more about these formats at the HTSQL website (`http://www.htsql.org`), and get a better idea of other methods of querying the data in your `control` database.

You have now successfully set up your Raspberry Pi to store data from the Arduino and made it accessible via HTSQL for viewing.

Summary

We demonstrated a simple method to write data to a database and to then be able to read it via our web browser. This combination of technologies leads us to all sorts of interesting possibilities. We could expand the SQLite3 database to hold more information on each of the rooms we plan to store data about, or we could expand our Python program to check whether the data being written to it is in the format we expect. We could also store humidity data.

HTSQL provides a variety of ways to write interesting queries that we can use in our web browser to check out our temperature readings. One of the benefits of HTSQL is that we can save these queries as bookmarks in our browser and use them whenever needed.

Hopefully, this chapter has generated interest in you to learn more about Python, HTSQL, and SQLite so that you can expand your home thermostat project further.

Next, we will look at setting up a parcel delivery detection device. We will be using the combination of the Arduino Uno and the Raspberry Pi to alert us via e-mail whenever a new package is delivered.

5
Parcel Delivery Detector

In this chapter, we are going to build a device that will sense and trigger once a parcel is delivered. This project will build upon our previous work of building the Raspberry Pi control device.

We will be editing the database that we created in the previous chapter to store information on deliveries. We will then query this data via HTSQL.

We will be also be adding a functionality that will allow the Raspberry Pi to send us e-mail alerts. This functionality will also form the basis for alerts in *Chapter 7, Water/Damp Detection – Check for Damp/Flooding in Sheds and Basements*.

For this project, you will need:

- An Arduino Uno
- An Ethernet shield
- A Cat-5 Ethernet cable
- A power adaptor/wall wart/battery pack
- A force-sensing resistor (pressure sensor)
- Wires
- A breadboard
- A 10K ohm resistor
- Your Raspberry Pi control device
- Waterproof casing
- A bin or box to place parcels in

Wiring up the parcel sensor

Our first task is to wire up the system. This will involve hooking up the Ethernet shield to the Arduino and then building a circuit to connect the force-based resistor to the Arduino's pins. To start with, we will briefly review what resistors are.

An introduction to resistors

A **resistor** is an electronic component with two connection points (known as terminals) that can be used to reduce the amount of electrical energy passing through a point in a circuit. This reduction in energy is known as resistance.

 Resistance is measured in **Ohms** (Ω).
You can read more about how this is calculated at
`http://en.wikipedia.org/wiki/Ohm's_law`.

You will find that resistors are usually classified into two groups,

- Fixed resistors: The fixed resistors that you will come across are usually made of a carbon film with the resistance marked in colored bands, giving you the value in ohms.

- Variable resistors: Components falling under the variable resistance group are those with resistance properties that change when some other ambient property or input in their environment changes. You will be exploring some of these throughout the book.

Let's now examine the two types of resistors we will be using in our circuit: a pressure sensor and a 10K ohm resistor.

Pressure sensor – force-sensing resistor

A **force-sensing resistor** (FSR) is a type of variable resistor. This means that if some input changes (pressure or force in our case), the resistance of the device also changes by a known amount. These types of resistors are perfect for testing whether somebody has placed a parcel onto a specific location.

10K ohm resistor

A **10K ohm**, unlike a pressure sensor, is designed to have a constant resistance, regardless of pressure, temperature, barometric change, or any other change. Resistors of this type fall under the fixed resistor category. You can tell the value of a resistor by examining the colored bands located on its body.

 When you purchase resistors, you may find they come with a color coding guide.

You can also check the chart on Wikipedia (http://en.wikipedia.org/wiki/Electronic_color_code#Resistor_color_coding) in order to ascertain what the value is.

You will need a 10K ohm resistor as a part of the circuit in order to detect the change in resistance while reading values from the analog pin.

Connecting the components to the Arduino

We are now ready to build the circuit and hardware for our parcel detector. To start with, take your Arduino Uno and attach the Ethernet shield to it. This will form a base to which we will be connecting other components.

Next, follow these steps to attach the force sensor, wires, and resistor:

- Take the breadboard and attach the force sensor to it.
- Take a wire. Attach one of its ends to the GRD pin on the Arduino and the other to the GRD on the breadboard so that it connects with the force sensor.
- Next, take another wire and attach one end to the 5V pin on the Arduino and the other end to the breadboard so that it connects to the power pin on the force sensor.
- We now need to attach the 10K ohm resistor. Attach this to the breadboard such that one leg is lined up with the GRD pin of the force sensor and the other is attached to the GND wire for the Arduino.
- Finally, attach a wire from A0 such that it connects to the GRD pin on the force sensor after the 10K ohm resistor.

The following diagram shows the setup:

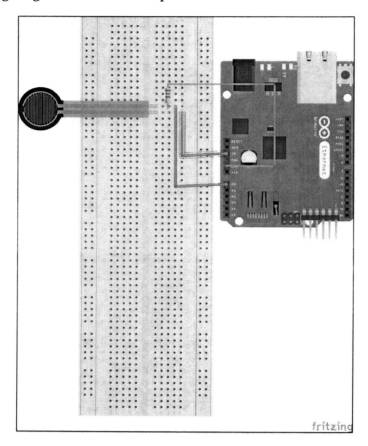

Writing our software

With the hardware ready, it is now time to write an Arduino sketch to test our circuit. This sketch will be responsible for checking when the forced-based resistor has enough pressure on it and then triggering an HTTP request.

Let's start by adding the include statements and variables to the sketch:

```
#include <SPI.h>
#include <Ethernet.h>
#define THRESHOLD 400

unsigned char fsr = 0; //The sensor pin
int check_pressure = 0;
int room = 2;
```

```
boolean is_delivered = true;
boolean email_sent = false;
byte mac[] = { 0xDE, 0xAD, 0xBB, 0xEF, 0xFE, 0xED };
char server[] = "192.168.3.4";
IPAddress ip(192,168,3,6);
EthernetClient client;
```

In the preceding code, we included the libraries we need. You should recognize these from *Chapter 3, Central Air and Heating Thermostat.*

Next, we define the fsr variable to record which analog pin we are using. The THRESHOLD, check_pressure, and is_delivered variables are used to test and record whether a package has been placed on the sensor.

The room variable is the ID of the room or location where the parcel sensor will be placed. Later in this chapter, we will add this room to our SQLite database on the Raspberry Pi.

Finally, you will see several variables used to define the IP address and MAC address of the Arduino, and the IP address of the Raspberry Pi. Remember to update these IP addresses to reflect your local network's addressing scheme.

Next, add the following functions:

```
void setup() {
  Serial.begin(9600);
  Ethernet.begin(mac, ip);
  pinMode(fsr, INPUT);
}

void loop() {
  check_pressure = analogRead(fsr);
  Serial.println(check_pressure);
  if(is_delivered) {
    if(check_pressure > THRESHOLD) {
      is_delivered = true;
      if(!email_sent){
        notify_parcel();
      }
      email_sent = true;
    }
  } else {
    if(check_pressure < THRESHOLD) {
      is_delivered = false; //reset system.
      email_sent = false;
      Serial.println(is_delivered);
```

```
        }
      }
  }
```

The `setup()` function is used to set the analog pin to input mode and to set up our Ethernet connection.

Next is the `loop()` function. This contains the code that checks whether the force sensor has enough pressure on it to trigger an HTTP request. Testing the result returned from the analog pin carries out this check. We then compare this result to the `THRESHOLD` constant, which we defined at the beginning of our sketch.

If the force exceeds the threshold, we set `is_delivered` to true and send an e-mail. We then disable sending e-mails by setting the `email_sent` variable to true. This prevents the system from constantly sending new e-mails.

When the parcel is removed from the sensor, the value returned from the analog pin dips below `THRESHOLD` and we then reset the system.

Finally, we need to add the code that sends the HTTP POST request to our Raspberry Pi. Paste the following code in your sketch:

```
void notify_parcel() {
    //update raspberry Pi
    String data = "{\"room\":";
    data += room;
    data += "}";
    if (client.connect(server, 8081)) {
      Serial.println("connected");
      client.println("POST / HTTP/1.1");
      client.println("Host: 192.168.3.6");
      client.println("Content-Type: application/json;charset=utf-8");
      client.print("Content-Length: ");
      client.println(data.length());
      client.println();
      client.println(data);
      client.println("Connection: close");
      client.println();
    }
    else {
      Serial.println("connection failed");
    }
}
```

The `notify_parcel()` function creates a simple HTTP post request containing some JSON data. This data consists of the ID of the room in which the parcel sensor is located.

The port number 8081 is where we are going to serve our Python web service to take this incoming HTTP request data and turn it into a DB query and e-mail.

Save the code and upload it to your Arduino.

This completes the Arduino sketch. Let's now turn our attention to the Raspberry Pi.

Updating the Raspberry Pi database

Our Arduino is now making HTTP requests when the pressure sensor is tripped. Therefore, we need to update the Raspberry Pi's database we created in the previous chapter to collect this information.

In order to write this data to the database, we will also need to create a small web service that captures the HTTP request and generates a SQL query.

We will start by updating our SQLite database to include a table to capture sensor data. Open `control.db` in SQLite and run the following query:

```
CREATE TABLE Parcel (ID INTEGER PRIMARY KEY AUTOINCREMENT, RoomIDINTEGER,
DatetimeDATETIME, FOREIGN KEY(RoomID) REFERENCES RoomDetails(ID));
```

This creates a new table called `Parcel`. In this table, we record where the parcel was delivered and the time stamp, and also create a unique ID for the parcel.

Currently, we have only one room in the database; this is where you placed your Arduino thermostat. We now need to insert the details of the room where the Arduino parcel sensor will be stored.

This will be where your packages are delivered; for example, it could be the porch, garage, or front step:

```
INSERT INTO RoomDetails (Room) VALUES ('Porch');
```

This completes the edits of the database. Now we can write the web service that will insert values into the `Parcel` table.

A web-based Python application

Python comes with a simple HTTP library that is perfect for creating a small web application. The web application, also known as a web service, is designed to provide a simple set of functionality: receive data, store it, and e-mail to confirm that it has received the data.

In *Chapter3, Central Air and Heating Thermostat,* we used the HTTP server functionality of the Arduino to query the thermostat for data. In this chapter, we will be reversing the actions, where the Arduino will be posting to the Raspberry Pi.

Setting up SMTP

We recommend using an external e-mail service and connecting to it.

While you can host an SMTP server on your Raspberry Pi, you may find spam blockers will prevent the email for reaching its target.

 SMTP stands for **Simple Mail Transfer Protocol**. An SMTP server is an application that handles sending e-mails on the device it is installed on, for example, the Raspberry Pi.

There are various choices of external e-mail services, including Gmail, GoDaddy, Hushmail and similar.

Services such as Gmail also offer inexpensive monthly services where you can register a domain name and link multiple e-mail accounts to it. This will allow you to assign an account to each device that sends e-mails if you wish. Of course, you can always use a single address and send e-mails to yourself!

You will need the following information from your e-mail provider:

- The SMTP service's address
- The SMTP service's port number
- Your account name
- Your account e-mail address

With this information, we can now write our Python web service and send e-mail updates when the parcel arrives.

Our Python application

The Python application that we are about to write will handle the incoming GET and POST requests, and will also be responsible for connecting to the SMTP server to send e-mails.

Log in to your Raspberry Pi and create a new file called `webservice.py`. This is where we are going to write our code.

Let's start by adding to the file the list of libraries we wish to import:

```
#!/usr/bin/env python
import sqlite3
import smtplib
import cgi
import json
from BaseHTTPServer import BaseHTTPRequestHandler,HTTPServer
from email.mime.text import MIMEText
```

Here, we will be importing the libraries that will handle the incoming HTTP requests, process the incoming JSON variables, and connect to our SQLite database.

Next, we will add to our file a class that handles the incoming HTTP GET and POST requests:

```
class RequestHandler(BaseHTTPRequestHandler):

    def do_GET(self):
        self.send_response(200)
        self.send_header('Content-type','text/html')
        self.end_headers()
        self.wfile.write("Parcel sensor service running!")
        return
```

Here, we handle an incoming GET request and respond with an HTML page to let the user know the system is up and running.

Next, let's add the code for handling the POST request:

```
    def do_POST(self):
        data_string = cgi.parse_qs(self.rfile.read(int(self.
headers['Content-Length'])), keep_blank_values=1)
        room = json.loads(data_string.keys()[0])['room']
        my_query = 'INSERT INTO parcel(roomid,datetime) \
                    VALUES(%s,CURRENT_TIMESTAMP);' %(room)


        try:
            connection = sqlite3.connect('/home/pi/control.
db',isolation_level=None)
            cursor = connection.cursor()
            cursor.execute(my_query)
            query_results = cursor.fetchone()
            my_response = "New parcel delivered to room ID %s" %
(room)
            self.send_mail()
```

```
    except sqlite3.Error, e:
        my_response = "There is an error %s:" % (e)
    finally:
        print my_response
        connection.close()
```

Here, we accept an incoming POST request and extract the room value that is passed to the web service. Next, we take this value and write it to the SQLite database with a timestamp.

After the query has been executed, we call the send_mail() function. Let's add this function next to our code:

```
def send_mail(self):
    sender = 'XXX@XXXX.com'
    receivers = ['XXX@XXXX.com']
    password = 'XXXXXX'
    fromad = 'Raspberry Pi Parcel Sensor <XXX@XXXX.com>'
    toad = 'Name <XXX@XXXX.com>'
    subject = 'A new parcel has been delivered'
    body = 'A new parcel was delivered.'
    msg = MIMEText(body)
    msg['From'] = fromad
    msg['To'] = toad
    msg['Subject'] = subject
```

We start the function by adding some variables that will be used to craft our e-mail. In this block of code, you will need to replace xxxx with your own values. This will include the SMTP details you collected earlier in this chapter, and the e-mail addresses you wish to send the parcel delivery alert to.

To this function, we will now add the code to actually send the e-mail:

```
try:
    smtp = smtplib.SMTP('XXXXX', 587)
    smtp.ehlo()
    smtp.starttls()
    smtp.ehlo
    smtp.login(sender, password)
    smtp.sendmail(sender, receivers, msg.as_string())
    print "Successfully sent email"
    smtp.close()
except smtplib.SMTPException:
    print "Error: unable to send email"
```

In this block of code, we use a `try` and `except` statement to send the e-mail. If it is successful, the code connects to our SMTP account and sends the e-mail. If it fails, we print a message to the terminal informing us that the e-mail could not be sent.

Let's add our final block of code:

```
class WebService():

    port = 8081

    def start_server(self):
        server = HTTPServer(('', self.port), RequestHandler)
        server.serve_forever()


if __name__ == "__main__":
    webservice = WebService()
    webservice.start_server()
```

Here, we start an HTTP service on port 8081. This is the port on your Raspberry Pi that the Arduino sketch connects to. This wraps up our web service. Save the file and exit.

We are now going to start the service.

Starting the web service

Starting the web service is simple; from the command line, run this expression:

pythonwebservice.py&

The application is now running on port 8081 and also as a background process on the Pi. You will notice that the process number will be displayed on the command line, for example, `[1] 10813`.

 The & symbol in the preceding command places the process in the background. To view this process, you can type `ps aux | grep "webservice.py"`.

You can test it by accessing the following URL: `http://<ip of raspberry pi>:8081`.

The Raspberry Pi will return the following response to the browser: `Parcel sensor service running!`

If you see a successful response, then your web service is running successfully.

> If you wish to stop the web service, you can kill the process using `kill <process number>`.

Testing our application

We are almost done with our parcel detection system. With the Arduino up and running and the Raspberry Pi setup complete, let's test our system.

You will need a book or some other object to represent a package:

1. Take the pressure sensor and place your book or object on it.

2. Run the following HTSQL query from your browser: `http://<ip of raspberry pi>:8080/parcel`.

3. You should now see an entry in your parcel table.

4. Next, check your e-mail. If your application is working successfully, you will have an e-mail sent from the Raspberry Pi.

Our system is now complete. We can install it so that it can be used with real-life parcel deliveries.

Installing the parcel detector

Now we have confirmed that our system is working. The next task will be to hook up the system to your home.

If you plan to place the system outside, you will need to ensure that it is covered so that it can be protected from the elements. There are a number of options to do this, such as:

- Purchasing an enclosure online. Companies such as Radio shack (`http://www.radioshack.com/search?q=enclosures#prefn1=productType&q=enclosures&prefv1=Project%20boxes`), Rapid, and Maplin offer a variety of project enclosures.

- Designing an enclosure and having Shapeways (`http://www.shapeways.com`) 3D-print it for you.

- Building your own enclosure from wood or plastic.

Once you have completed or purchased the enclosure, you will need a box, a small bin or trash can, or something similar for the parcels to be placed in.

Install your parcel detection device in the box. If the enclosure allows for it, you may want to attach it to the side of the box, ensuring that the FRS is located at the bottom of the box.

As a power source, you can use either a standard 12V DC power adapter or a battery power pack. If you use an adapter, you may need to use an extension cord as well.

Since we are using Ethernet, you will also need to drill or cut a hole for the cable to run through. You can then run the Ethernet cable to your switch or hub.

Some Ethernet shields come with **Power over Ethernet (PoE)**. This is a great option if your shield supports it, and it will save you on batteries.

PoE modules can also be purchased and soldered on your circuit, they can be found at the Arduino store, at `http://store. arduino.cc/product/X000002`.

Finally, place a mat over the sensor. This should be light enough so as not to trigger the system. The following diagram will illustrate the layout of the installation:

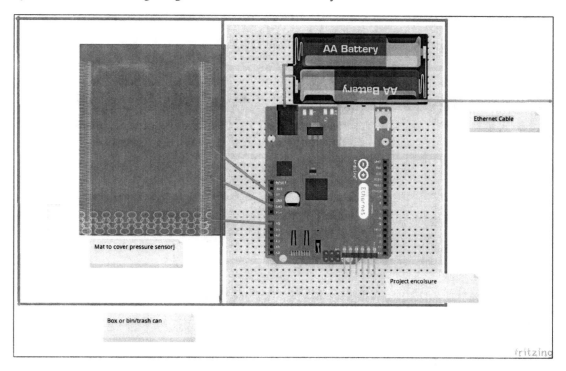

This completes the system installation.

Testing the complete setup

Our system is now installed and ready to go. Our final task will be to test the system again to confirm that we have installed it correctly.

The battery pack or power adapter should be hooked up to power your Arduino. Ensure that its lights are on. After this, try the following steps:

1. Place a heavy object in the parcel delivery box.
2. From a separate computer, run the following HTSQL query: `http://<iphttp://<ip of rrp>:8080/parcel`.
3. You should see an entry with a timestamp for now.
4. Next, check your e-mail account. If you get an e-mail, this confirms that your setup works.

Congratulations! You now have a working, installed parcel detection system. Let's consider some steps to improve the project further.

Next steps

There is a range of features we can add to the system to expand its functionality. Each of these has been listed here.

Upgrading from Ethernet to a wireless system

Attaching an Ethernet cable to your system may be inconvenient for a number of reasons. Therefore, we could upgrade the system to use wireless technology. One popular choice is XBee.

You can read more about XBee at `http://www.digi.com/xbee/`.
There is also further information on using XBee with the Arduino Wireless shield, at `http://arduino.cc/en/Main/ArduinoWirelessShield`.

Checking the shipping details

Currently, we don't know which parcel has been delivered. Therefore, it would be useful to log into a shipping website to check which parcel has arrived.

A useful Python library called `packagetrack` is available for this purpose. It can be found at `https://pypi.python.org/pypi/packagetrack/0.2`.

With this package installed, you can import it to your Python application. The web service can then log into UPS, for example, and retrieve the shipping details.

Replacing the pressure sensor with a camera and image recognition

Checking for a parcel with a pressure sensor is good, but how about improving on this? We could replace the sensor with a camera module that uses image processing to check whether a package has been delivered, and then e-mails a photo of it to us.

One option to achieve this is the Pixy cam from Charmed Labs:
http://charmedlabs.com/default/?page_id=211

Using this module hooked up to the Arduino, we can check whether a parcel-like object has been delivered to a location within the view of the camera, and trigger the HTTP request.

 Further information on the Pixy cams software and setup can found at http://cmucam.org/projects/cmucam5/wiki.

This wraps up the next steps section, let's review what we have learned in this chapter.

Summary

In this chapter, we built a package-detecting system and built upon the work completed in earlier chapters. We designed a circuit and attached it to the Arduino. This circuit recorded if a package was placed on a sensor.

When a parcel was detected, an HTTP POST request was made to the Raspberry Pi. Then the Raspberry Pi, through a web service, placed a timestamp and the location where the parcel was delivered in our SQLite database.

Following this, it sent an e-mail to alert us that the parcel had arrived. Next, we took our completed system and installed it so that it was ready for use in our home, and wrapped up with some ideas on improvements.

In the next chapter, we will build a system to open and close curtains based on the light in the room. For this, we will be using the Raspberry Pi to Arduino bridge shield.

6

Curtain Automation – Open and Close the Curtains Based on the Ambient Light

In this chapter, we will be looking at how to use a photoresistor and a motor shield in conjunction with our Raspberry Pi. Once these are combined into a single device, it can be used to open and close blinds or curtains. We will also introduce the use of the Arduino to Raspberry Pi connection bridge shield.

You will need the following for this chapter:

- The Raspberry Pi
- The Arduino to Raspberry Pi connection bridge shield
- A breadboard
- Wires
- resistor
- A photoresistor
- An Arduino motor shield
- A 9V battery and a battery connector
- A flathead screwdriver
- A flashlight
- A 9V DC motor and an optional 12V DC motor
- A 12V wall wart if you use a 12V motor

Introduction to the Arduino bridge shield

In this chapter, we will be using the Arduino bridge shield. We already introduced the Arduino bridge shield in *Chapter 2, Getting Started – Setting Up Your Raspberry Pi and Arduino*.

In the past, you used an Arduino microcontroller connected to your Raspberry Pi over the Ethernet. With the Cooking Hacks bridge shield, we can use our Raspberry Pi for direct interaction with Arduino shields. This provides us with an option of writing Arduino programs on the Raspberry Pi and reusing the existing shield hardware that we purchased. Therefore, your Raspberry Pi control unit can also double up as a microcontroller-like device to interact with your home when you connect the hardware to its GPIO pins.

To start writing applications that can harness the bridge shield, you need to install the arduPi library made by Cooking Hacks. This library will allow us to write Arduino-like applications and run them on the Raspberry Pi.

Installing arduPi

Open the terminal window on your Raspberry Pi, create a new directory in which you will install the arduPi library, and then navigate to it:

```
mkdir arduPi
cd arduPi
```

1. Using wget, download the library from the command line:

   ```
   wget http://www.cooking-hacks.com/skin/frontend/default/cooking/
   images/catalog/documentation/raspberry_arduino_shield/arduPi_1-5.
   tar.gz
   ```

   After wget has run, a tar.gz file will be saved in the current directory.

2. From the terminal, run the following command. This will extract the entire zipped-up file. The <revision version> will be specific to the tar.gz file you downloaded:

   ```
   tar xzf arduPi_<revision version>.tar.gz
   ```

   In our case, this will be version 1.5. Thus, you need to type this command to extract the file:

   ```
   tar xzf arduPi_rev1-5.tar.gz
   ```

3. Once the file has finished extracting, you will find three new files in the directory. Type the following command to list the directory's contents:

```
ls
```

4. You will now see the `arduPi.cpp`, `arduPi.h`, and `arduPi_template.cpp` files:

   ° The `arduPi.cpp` and `arduPi.h` files contain code that will be used to provide support for interaction with your Arduino to Raspberry Pi shield.

   ° The `arduPi_template.cpp` file provides a basic template file. You can use this file to create applications. You might notice that it looks very similar to a basic Arduino sketch.

5. In order to use the `arduPi_template.cpp` file, we need to compile the `arduPi.cpp` file into an object file. For this task, we will be using a C++ compiler.

6. To compile the C++ code, we type the following:

```
g++ -c arduPi.cpp -o arduPi.o
```

This command invokes the `g++` compiler, takes the `arduPi.cpp` as an input file, and outputs an object file called `arduPi.o`.

Now that we have the code compiled, we can look at hooking up our hardware and writing some software to control a circuit. We will start by reviewing the hardware we need.

Photoresistors

A photoresistor is similar to the thermistor in that the device's resistance changes as some ambient property of the room changes. With the thermistor, this property was temperature; with the photoresistor, it is light.

The most common application of photoresistors that you see in everyday life is in street lamps, which switch on when it starts to get dark outside.

We can use a photoresistor as a part of our circuit to tell when it is getting dark outside, and send this information to the Raspberry Pi. The Raspberry Pi can then process this data and use it to control an electric motor.

Motor shield and motors

For this project, we choose the official Arduino motor shield. This is a device that we can connect to our Raspberry Pi to Arduino shield. Then we can use it to attach and drive DC motors.

The specifications for the shield can be found at http://arduino.cc/en/Main/ArduinoMotorShieldR3.

The shield has an operating voltage in the range of 5V to 12V. For our project, we will connect a 9V battery to the screw terminal power connectors.

For testing purposes, we will use a 9V battery. However, if you wish to install the motor-shield based-device, you should consider attaching it to a wall wart or mains adapter. A 9V battery in constant use will not last very long and will not power a 12V motor.

It is recommended that you disconnect the power pins on the shield if you wish to connect devices that require more than 9V.

We will start this project using a 9V motor. You can always upgrade to a 12V motor once you have your application and circuit up and running.

Depending on the type of blinds you have, using a motor in the range of 9V to 12V should provide enough torque.

Setting up the photoresistor

We are going to start by wiring up our photoresistor and testing it with software that uses the arduPi library. Once we have tested it, we can hook it up with the motor shield and use the values it returns to turn the motor on and off.

Wiring up the components

Our first task is to set up our circuit. This process is very similar to the way you created the FSR circuit in *Chapter 5, Parcel Delivery Detector*.

You'll need your resistor, photoresistor, three wires (black, red, and yellow are used in the explanation), and the breadboard. Follow these steps to wire up the components:

- Take the red wire and connect it from the 5V pin on the shield to the supply voltage on the breadboard.
- Next, connect the black wire from the ground pin on the Raspberry Pi to Arduino bridge shield to the ground on the breadboard.

- As we did with the FSR circuit before, we will now connect a resistor to the breadboard. Connect one pin of your resistor to the supply voltage strip that your red wire is connected to, and then connect the other end to a terminal strip.

- We can now connect our photoresistor. Insert one leg of the photoresistor into the ground on the bus strip, and place the second leg into the same row as you placed the resistor.

- Finally, connect one end of your yellow wire from the **analog 7 (A7)** pin on your shield to the terminal strip you selected.

The following diagram will help you to understand the layout:

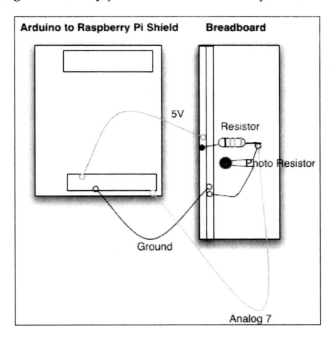

Now that we have the hardware in place, we can write an application to test our setup.

Testing the photoresistor with software

We will be using the arduPi template we installed earlier to create our test code.

Take a copy of arduPi_template.cpp and rename it as LightSensor.cpp.

Next, in a text editor of your choice, open the new file and add the following code to it:

```
//Include ArduPi library
#include "arduPi.h"
//Include the Math library
#include <math.h>

#define TH 690
```

Here, we had the standard template header, but we also added a new constant called TH. This will represent the threshold. Like the setpoint constant we declared for the thermostat, the threshold is used to decide to perform an operation based upon whether the room gets lighter or darker.

Let's move on to add the next block of code. Paste this block after the previous code you added to your file:

```
/**********************************************************
 *   IF YOUR ARDUINO CODE HAS OTHER FUNCTIONS APART FROM  *
 *   setup() AND loop() YOU MUST DECLARE THEM HERE        *
 *   *****************************************************/

/************************
 * YOUR ARDUINO CODE HERE *
 * **********************/


int main (){
  setup();
  while(1){
    loop();
  }
 return (0);
}


void setup(void) {
}

void loop(void) {


float analogReadingArduino;
analogReadingArduino = analogRead(7);
```

Here, we set up analog pin 7 so that we can read the values returned by the photoresistor.

Next, let's add the following code. This displays a message depending on whether the photoresistor is detecting more or less light:

```
if(analogReadingArduino > TH ){
        printf("Getting lighter\n");
} else{
        printf("Getting darker\n");
}

delay(3000);
}
```

As you can see in the `if` statement, we check whether light falling on the photoresistor is greater than the threshold value. If it is, then the program displays the `Getting lighter` message. Otherwise, it displays the `Getting darker` message. Save the file and exit. Following this, we will look at a method used to compile our code so that we can run it.

Makefiles

The next tool that we are going to use is a Makefile. A Makefile is executed by the `make` Linux command. The `make` command is a command-line utility that allows you to compile executable files by storing the parameters in a Makefile and then calling it as needed. This method allows us to store common compilation directives and reuse them without having to type the command each time.

So create the following Makefile using a text editor of your choice:

```
Photo: arduPi.o
  g++ -lrt -lpthread LightSensor.cpp arduPi.o -o lightsensor
```

Once the Makefile is complete, save the file and run `make` from the command line in the same directory as your code:

```
make
```

From the command line, we can now test the code, like this:

```
./lightsensor
```

Now that the application is running, we can try out our photoresistor. Depending on the ambient light in the room, you will see the **Getting lighter** or **Getting darker** message.

If you see the **Getting darker** message, try shining your flashlight on the sensor. Once the threshold is passed, the message will change to **Getting lighter**.

If you see the **Getting lighter** message first, you can try placing a finger over the sensor, and once the threshold is passed, the message will change to **Getting darker**.

Setting up the motor shield

The first part of the circuit is now complete. We have a device that can record the change in light and can send this information to our application via an analog pin.

Now we need to connect our photoresistor to the motor shield. Once these are connected, we will have a device that can be used to control curtains or blinds.

Let's start by setting up our hardware.

Wiring the components to the shield

Unlike previous steps, we will be making some small modifications to an Arduino shield. Our motor shield uses pins 11 through 13, but the Raspberry Pi already has these pins set aside for SPI. This means that we will need to disable some of the current pins on the motor shield. You will also need to use your flathead screwdriver for some of these steps:

- Unplug the red, black, and yellow wires that connect your breadboard to the Raspberry Pi to Arduino shield.

- Bend the metal legs on digital pins numbered 4, 5, 6, 11, 12, and 13. You do not need to remove the legs; just ensure that they will not connect with the header on the bridge shield.

- You can connect the motor shield to the Raspberry Pi to Arduino shield. We will now run some jumper wires to connect digital pins 11, 12, and 13 on the motor shield to digital pins 4, 5, and 6 on the Raspberry Pi to Arduino shield, respectively. Take your jumper wires and connect 11 to 4, 12 to 5, and 13 to 6.

- Our two shields are now wired together. Next, connect two wires to the A terminal on your shield; you will need a small, flathead screwdriver in order to open and close the connection. Once these are in place, join your battery connector to the ground and power connectors. Ensure that the black wire connects to negative and the red wire to positive.

- Next, connect your electric motor to the two wires connected to the A terminal. This completes the motor shield setup.

- We can now reconnect our photoresistor. Connect the red wire to a 5V power pin, the black back to a ground pin, and finally, the yellow wire to the analog 7 pin.

Our circuit is now complete. Let's take a look at how we can make it work with a DC motor.

Curtain control application

We will now write an application that leverages the photoresistor and uses it to control the motor. There are a few concepts that we will cover quickly before we write the application, in order to provide you with better understanding of how our software works.

Pulse width modulation

Pulse width modulation (PWM) is a method that leverages the digital pins to create an analog result. If a digital pin is switched on, it has a value of 5V, and if switched off, it has a value of 0V. PWM allows us to simulate a value between these two ends.

Using our software, we can create what is known as a square wave. This method involves switching a pin on and off to create a signal to the device connected to the digital pin. In our project, it's a DC motor. Therefore, varying the modulation (that is, changing the number of milliseconds that the pin is switched off versus on) will result in a change of speed of the DC motor.

In order to create PWM in our application, we will need to use threads. We will look at these next.

Threads

You may have noticed that when running our Makefile, the compilation directives include a reference to -lpthread.

The pthread library allows us to create threaded applications. A thread is essentially a fork in the program that can continue to run while the application performs other tasks.

In the context of our program, this allows us to generate PWM outside the loop() function, which will run continuously until we tell it otherwise.

Consider the `setup()` function. In it, we can create a thread that generates PWM on pin 3 of the shield. In the `loop()` function, we can perform other tasks, pause the PWM thread, update the values used to generate PWM, and restart it. These new values will then be used in the PWM thread.

You will see this concept in action next in our curtain control application.

Writing our code

Let's take the light sensor code we wrote, and expand it to start controlling the motor shield.

Start up your favorite text editor and create a new file called `CurtainControl.cpp`. Add the following code to this file:

```
//Include ArduPi library
#include "arduPi.h"

#define TH 690
#define DIRECTION 5
#define PWMPIN 3
```

Here, we have our standard template headers and the threshold we defined in `LightSensor.cpp`. After this, we have added two new constants, `DIRECTION` and `PWMPIN`.

 The TH value will depend on a number of variables, the type of photoresistor used, the resistor used, and location of the device. Therefore, you may need to experiment and tweak this value for the location and components you use.

The `DIRECTION` constant stores the pin on the motor shield. that is used to define which way the motor is running, clockwise or counterclockwise.

We use the `PWMPIN` constant to store the pin number of the pin on which we create a square wave (PWM). Now add the following code:

```
pthread_t pwmthread;
pthread_mutex_t pwmmutex = PTHREAD_MUTEX_INITIALIZER;
```

These declarations are used for the thread that we will be generated when we create PWM on pin 3. The thread is stored under the variable name of `pwmthread`. Next, we add two Boolean variables that act as flags:

```
boolean off_on;
boolean open_state;
```

The first variable is used to store the condition of the motor (switched on or off), and the second variable records the open or closed state of our blinds:

```
/******************************************************
 *  IF YOUR ARDUINO CODE HAS OTHER FUNCTIONS APART FROM  *
 *  setup() AND loop() YOU MUST DECLARE THEM HERE        *
 *  ****************************************************/

/*************************
 * YOUR ARDUINO CODE HERE *
 * **********************/

void* pwm(void *args) {

  while(1){

    if(off_on == true) {
      digitalWrite(3, HIGH);
      delayMicroseconds(100);
      digitalWrite(3, LOW);
      delayMicroseconds(1000 - 100);
    } else {
      digitalWrite(3, LOW);
    }

  }
  return NULL;
}
```

This function is concerned with the process of generating pulse width modulation. The `while` loop runs indefinitely, and the code within it is responsible for switching pin 3 between `HIGH` and `LOW` with a pause between each command to control the speed.

There is a conditional statement that checks whether the motor should be switched on or off. If the variable is set to `false`, then it means that the curtain is either fully open or shut. Thus, we switch the voltage applied to pin 3 to 0 (`LOW`).

Next, we need a function to control the motor's state. This function pauses the thread, updates the on/off state, and then restarts the thread:

```
void controlMotor(boolean state) {
  pthread_mutex_lock( &pwmmutex );
  off_on=state;
  pthread_mutex_unlock( &pwmmutex );
}
```

This allows us to switch off the PWM at any point in our application, which in turn stops the motor:

```
int main(void) {
  setup();
  while(1){
    loop();
    delay(100);
  }
  return 0;
}
```

```
void setup(){

  pthread_create(&(pwmthread), NULL, &pwm,  NULL);
  pinMode(DIRECTION, OUTPUT);
 }
```

We added two new statements to the setup() function. The first statement creates the new PWM thread, and the second sets the direction pin stored in the DIRECTION constant to OUTPUT:

```
void loop(){


  float analogReadingArduino;
  analogReadingArduino = = analogRead(7);
```

Next, we need to add code that uses the data generated by the photoresistor on A7:

```
if(analogReadingArduino > TH && open_state == false){
  controlMotor(true);
  digitalWrite(DIRECTION, HIGH);
  delay(5000);
  open_state = true;
  controlMotor(false);
} else{
  if(analogReadingArduino < TH && open_state == true){

    controlMotor(true);
    digitalWrite(DIRECTION, LOW);
    delay(5000);
    open_state = false;
    controlMotor(false);
  }
}
```

Here, we have a conditional statement that checks the light readings against the TH (threshold) constant. If the curtains are shut and the light exceeds the threshold, then we do the following:

1. Call the controlMotor() function and pass the Boolean value of true.

2. Switch pin 5 to HIGH, which sets the direction of the motor to clockwise.

3. Allow the motor to run for 5 seconds in order to open the curtain.

4. Call the controlMotor() function and pass the Boolean value of false, which turns the motor off.

Let's now look at the next part of the if statement.

Here, we check whether the reading from A7 is less than the threshold and whether the curtains are open. If both are true, it means the room is darkening, and the blinds need to be closed:

1. Once again, we call the controlMotor() function and switch the motor on.

2. Next, the direction of the motor is set to counterclockwise by writing LOW to digital pin 5.

3. Then we apply a 5-second delay to allow the blinds to close fully.

4. Finally, we switch the motor off.

This wraps up the application. We can now test it against our circuit.

1. Create a Makefile for the curtain control application in your text editor, and add the following directives:

```
Curtain: arduPi.o
    g++ -lrt -lpthread CurtainControl.cpp arduPi.o -o curtaincontrol
```

2. Run the make command from the command line. Then start the application:

```
./curtaincontrol
```

Now your curtain control application should be running. If you try changing the light on the photoresistor, you will notice that the motor changes direction and eventually stops.

Applying less and more light will cause the values returned by the photoresistor to pass the threshold, and thus switch the motor on and off, respectively.

Connecting to your blinds/curtains

The final step is to connect your motor to your blinds or curtain hardware. This will largely depend on the product you are using, and remember that heavy curtain and blind hardware will require a higher torque motor. You may wish to switch over to a 12V motor at this point.

 If you connect the 12V power supply and motor, remember to disconnect the power pins on the motor shield.

Let's now look at the delay values that we have to set in the loop() function.

Setting the timing

Our application has a delay of 5 seconds in the conditional statement that opens and closes the blinds. This was an arbitrary amount we set when creating our application. When you attach your motor to the blinds or curtains, you will need to calculate the number of seconds required to open and shut them. You can also adjust the values in the pwm() function to either speed up or slow down your motor.

Once you have set up the hardware, try experimenting with these values until you adjust the settings to your preference. For example, you may decide you never want the blinds fully closed or open, and can adjust the setting so that the closed and open state is 75 percent of the open and closed state of the physical curtain.

Attaching the hardware

At this point, you will need to attach the DC motor to the curtain drawstring. The preferred method of doing this is by using a pulley.

A variety of grooved pulleys can be found online or in hardware and craft stores. Select a pulley that fits the profile of your hardware.

 Make sure you are not running the curtain control application while attempting to attach the wheel and blinds, as this may make things difficult.

Attach the wheel to the axle of your DC motor. It should fit snuggly so that it does not fall off when the motor is switched on. Try testing your configuration by launching the `curtaincontrol` program.

Once you are sure this works, you can attach the drawstrings of your curtains or blinds to the wheel. This setup will largely depend on how the blinds are opened or closed. Commonly, there is a drawstring loop that can be pulled to open or close the blinds. This loop should be wound around the groove of the pulley wheel and fit tightly.

Now try changing the delay value in your application to 1 second. Next, run the `make` command again to recompile the application. Our application will now run the open/close cycle for 1 second. Execute the application via the command line and note how far the curtain/blind will open/close in 1 second.

With this information, you should be able to estimate how many seconds are required to open and close your hardware. At this point, you can try refining the numbers until you reach the desired result.

Debugging problems

If the curtains aren't opening and shutting, there could be one of the several problems listed here. We have listed some steps you can take to debug the problem:

- Ensure that the pulley wheel is attached tightly to the axle
- Ensure that the drawstring is attached to the pulley wheel and is tight enough to maintain its grip when the motor starts
- If the motor is facing problems opening the blinds and you are using a 9V motor, try upgrading to the 12V motor
- If the curtains are opening or shutting too quickly, adjust the delay as described earlier in the chapter

You now have an application and circuit that can control your curtains or blinds based on the ambient light in the room.

 Remember to check the tension of the drawstring as it may change over time and affect the accuracy of your open and close settings.

Next steps

Now we have a simple curtain control device up and running in our room. Let's look at some of the next steps.

Mounting the photoresistor outdoors

You may have noticed that turning the lights on in the room trips the light sensor, which is not good. Therefore, it would make sense to mount the photoresistor outside the house if you haven't done that already.

Your circuit should be easy to modify to include this feature. All you will need to do is extend the length of the wires connecting the photoresistor to the bridge shield.

These wires could then be fed through a window, allowing the Raspberry Pi to be stored inside so that it can be connected to the blinds.

Adding a stepper motor

Another motor type we could consider using is a DC stepper motor. A stepper motor divides a full revolution into an equal number of steps. The motor can then be controlled to move through each of these steps and paused at a certain step if needed.

Therefore, you can incrementally wind the curtain cord using this method.

 The Adafruit website provides a wide variety of stepper motor equipment, including mountings and brackets, at https://www.adafruit.com/search?g=1&q=stepper%20motor.

Adding a stepper motor will give you far more flexibility over the curtain control process than a simple DC motor, and it is an interesting method of upgrading your project.

Summary

This chapter introduced several new concepts, including pulse width modulation and using threads in our application. You also learned how to use a photoresistor and read the values from it.

Another important step we performed was modifying our motor shield. This provided an introduction to doctoring off-the-shelf Arduino shields to work with the Raspberry Pi.

Next, we will examine how we can build a damp and water detection system. This will incorporate both the Arduino Uno and the Raspberry Pi.

Using this device, we can know whether high humidity has been detected (which can be a sign of damp), and send an alert to the Raspberry Pi to inform us that we potentially have a problem.

7
Water/Damp Detection – Check for Damp/Flooding in Sheds and Basements

In the previous chapter, you learned how to control blinds and curtains. In this chapter, we will be building a damp detection device. This will bring together some of the ideas from other chapters and teach you the next steps used to expand the system.

The purpose of the damp detection device is to alert you when an area becomes damp or is at risk of flooding. A common method of checking for signs of flooding and dampness is to run a damp heat test. This involves checking a combination of temperature and humidity to see whether an area is susceptible to dampness, for example, if some insulation has become wet.

For this project we will use:

- The Raspberry Pi
- The Raspberry Pi to Arduino bridge shield
- An Ethernet shield
- An LED
- An Arduino Uno
- The AM2302 sensor
- The Seeed Grove water sensor

A brief note on dampness

Dampness in basements and sheds can lead to long-term damage, cause mold to grow, and also be an indication of flooding.

 The US CDC website at http://www.cdc.gov/mold/dampness_facts.htm recommends that humidity levels should be kept at about 50 percent in order to prevent molds from growing.

Therefore, it stands to reason that a high humidity level in a basement may be a sign of a problem. Thus, checking humidity levels will be a major factor in our damp and flooding detection device.

Let's get started with building the damp detection system.

Damp detection system

In this project, we will build a thermometer and a humidity sensor using an Arduino Uno and the AM230. This device will write the recorded data to the Raspberry Pi and store it in our control database.

Once we have this system up and running, we will look at some ideas on how we can expand the damp detection system to use the Cooking Hacks shield.

Let's start with building the Arduino circuit.

Arduino circuit

Our damp detection system is scalable, so we can build multiple damp detection units, and place them in separate locations such as the shed and the basement.

The Arduino thermometer/humidity circuit is the same as what we built for the thermostat. The following diagram illustrates it:

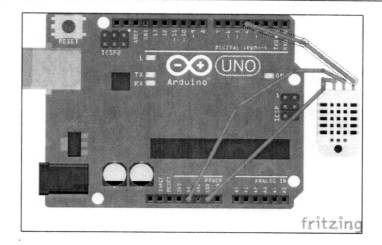

Building the circuit is simple, and you should be familiar with it by now. Attach your Ethernet shield to the Uno and then simply hook up the AM2302 to digital pin 4, the 5V pin, and the GRD pin. This completes the device's setup.

Now that we have built the circuit, let's write the Arduino software.

Sketch code

The following sketch is a simplified version of the code that we wrote in *Chapter 3, Central Air and Heating Thermostat*. In this code, we do not need to include a `setpoint` as we did with the thermostat.

Create a new sketch and add the following code to it:

```
#include "DHT.h"
#include <SPI.h>
#include <Ethernet.h>
#define DHTPIN 4 // The digital pin to read from
#define DHTTYPE DHT22 // DHT 22 (AM2302)

int room = 3;
```

Later in this chapter, we will add a new value to the room table in our SQLite database. The ID of this new room will be the value you will assign to the room variable in the preceding block of code. Then add the following:

```
byte mac[] = { 0xDE, 0xAD, 0xBE, 0xEF, 0xFE, 0xED };
IPAddress ip(192,168,3,6);
DHT dht(DHTPIN, DHTTYPE);
EthernetServer server(80);
EthernetClient client;

void setup() {
  Serial.begin(9600);
  Ethernet.begin(mac, ip);
  server.begin();
  dht.begin();
}

void loop() {
  float h = dht.readHumidity();
  float t = dht.readTemperature();

  // listen for incoming clients
  client = server.available();
  if (client) {
    // an http request ends with a blank line
    boolean currentLineIsBlank = true;
    String result;
    while (client.connected()) {
      if (client.available()) {
        char c = client.read();
        result= result + c;
      }

      if(result.indexOf("text/html") > -1) {
        client.println("HTTP/1.1 200 OK");
        client.println("Content-Type: text/html");
        client.println();
        if (isnan(h) || isnan(t)) {
          client.println("Failed to read from DHT sensor!");
          return;
        }
        client.println("Humidity: ");
        client.println(h);
        client.println(" %\t");
```

```
      client.println("<br />Temperature: ");
      client.println(t);
      client.println(" degrees C ");
      break;
   }

   if( result.indexOf("application/json") > -1 ) {
      client.println("HTTP/1.1 200 OK");
      client.println("Content-Type: application/
json;charset=utf-8");
      client.println("Server: Arduino");
      client.println("Connnection: close");
      client.println();
      client.print("{\"thermostat\":[{\"location\":\"");
      client.print(room);
      client.print("\"},");
      client.print("{\"temperature\":\"");
      client.print(t);
      client.print("\"},");
      client.print("{\"humidity\":\"");
      client.print(h);
      client.print("\"}");
      client.print("]}");
      client.println();
      break;
      }
   }
   delay(1);
   client.stop();
   }
}
```

Once you have uploaded the sketch to the Arduino, hook it up to your home network. If you connect from your browser to its IP address (192.168.3.6 in our example), you should see the humidity and temperature results:

Humidity: 35.70 %

Temperature: 14.90 degrees C

Next, we need to update the SQLite DB to include a column for humidity. Once we have this in place, we can record the value returned from the Arduino Uno.

Database updates

On your Raspberry Pi, use the following command to connect to the SQLite3 database that you created in *Chapter 4, Temperature Storage – Setting Up a Database to Store Your Results*:

```
sqlite3 control.db
```

We are now going to add a humidity column. Run the following SQL statement:

```
ALTER TABLE Temperature ADD COLUMN Humidity FLOAT(8);
```

This code modifies the temperature table and adds a humidity column. The column is set to accept values in float format. Next, we need to add the basement/shed to our room table:

```
INSERT INTO RoomDetails (Room) VALUES ('Basement');
```

 Remember to update the Arduino sketch with the ID of the room you insert.

Now we have a place to store the humidity data. Next, we need to create a new version of the request.py code from *Chapter 4, Temperature Storage – Setting Up a Database to Store Your Results*, to write the value to the database.

Python code

The following Python code is a modified version of the request.py code that we used previously.

Create a new file, damp.py, in a text editor of your choice and add the following code. Remember to change the IP address given here to that of your Arduino:

```python
#!/usr/bin/env python
import sqlite3
import urllib2
import json

def main():
    req = urllib2.Request('http://192.168.3.6/')
    req.add_header('Content-Type', 'application/json;charset=utf-8')
    r = urllib2.urlopen(req)
    result = json.load(r)
    room = result['thermostat'][0]['location']
    temperature = result['thermostat'][1]['temperature']
```

```
    humidity = result['thermostat'][1]['humidity']
    my_query = 'INSERT INTO temperature(roomid,temperaturec,datetime,
humidity) \
              VALUES(%s,%s,CURRENT_TIMESTAMP);' %(room,temperature,
humidity)
```

Here, we can see that we are storing the humidity value returned in the json object in a variable called humidity.

Next, we insert this value into the query that writes the data to our SQLite database:

```
    try:
        connection = sqlite3.connect('/home/pi/control.db',isolation_
level=None)
        cursor = connection.cursor()
        cursor.execute(my_query)
        query_results = cursor.fetchone()
        my_response = 'Inserted %s and %s for room %s' % (temperature,
humidity, room)
    except sqlite3.Error, e:
        my_response = "There is an error %s:" % (e)
    finally:
        connection.close()

if __name__ == "__main__":
    main()
```

Our final edit to the code is to modify the response message to output the humidity value. With our code in place, we can set up a second cron job to execute the Python application on an hourly basis.

Adding a cron job

Let's edit the crontab. Run the following command:

```
crontab -e
```

We want to take a reading once every hour, as we did with the thermostat. To do this, add the following code to your cron table:

```
0 * * * python damp.py
```

Save the file and then exit. Once the cron job has been executed, you can test whether the humidity data is being written by checking the database via HTSQL, at http://localhost:8080/temperature.

If you are not running the query from your Raspberry Pi, you will have to replace `localhost` with the IP address of your device.

You should now see the `humidity` column present, with a `humidity` value inserted into it. This wraps up the Arduino damp-detecting device and the changes required to the Raspberry Pi. Let's take a look at a few more ways of using this data.

Using the humidity reading

We now have a system that reads the humidity of the room in which the Arduino is located. Based on the temperature and humidity data, we can get to know whether the room is damp or there is a chance of flooding.

It would also be useful though, if the Raspberry Pi could alert us in some manner that the room is experiencing high humidity. Perhaps, we could use this data to turn on a dehumidifier.

Adding an LED alert

We are going to start by attaching the Cooking Hacks shield to the Raspberry Pi. Once this is connected, we will attach an LED to the shield's digital pin 2. The following diagram illustrates the setup:

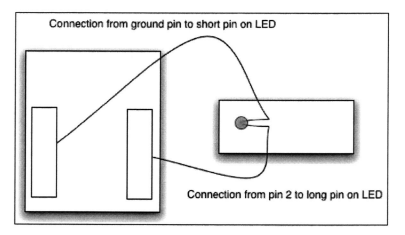

Connect the long pin of the LED to digital pin 2 on the Arduino bridge shield. You can use a breadboard and two wires in order to complete this setup. Next, attach the other leg of the LED to the GRD pin on the bridge shield.

Once you have the LED attached, you can consider writing an application to switch it on and off.

Blinking LED code

The following application causes the LED to blink, and it is very simple to implement:

1. Create a new file on the Raspberry Pi, in the same directory as your curtain control application. Name it `alert.cpp`:

```
touch alert.cpp
```

   We will use the `arduPi` template as a base for this application as well.

2. Open the file in your text editor of choice. Start by adding the following code:

```
//Include ArduPi library
#include "arduPi.h"


/**********************************************************
 *   IF YOUR ARDUINO CODE HAS OTHER FUNCTIONS APART FROM  *
 *   setup() AND loop() YOU MUST DECLARE THEM HERE        *
 *   ****************************************************/


/*************************
 * YOUR ARDUINO CODE HERE *
 * **********************/

int main (){
  setup();
  while(1){
    loop();
  }
  return (0);
}
```

   This block of code is the standard `arduPi` template that tells the application to run in a loop.

3. We now need to add some code to switch pin 2 to the OUTPUT mode so that we can switch the LED on and off. Add the following block of code to `alert.cpp`:

```
void setup(){
  pinMode(2,OUTPUT);
}
```

4. The `setup()` function is responsible for switching the pin mode to output. Next, we will add the code that will cause the LED to blink to the `loop()` function:

```
void loop() {

digitalWrite(2,HIGH);
delay(1000);
digitalWrite(2,LOW);
delay(1000);

}
```

Here, we switch pin 2 between `HIGH` and `LOW` with a 1-second pause. This creates the blinking effect.

5. We can now compile and test the application. Exit the text editor and run the following command:

```
g++ -lrt -lpthread alert.cpp arduPi.o -o alert
```

 Remember that you can add this to a Makefile.

6. The compiled alert program can be run from the command line:

```
./alert
```

You should now see the LED blinking on and off with a 1-second interval. This program forms the basics of an alert system that will trigger the LED when damp is detected. However, we need a way to know when to switch the LED alert on and off. We will look at this next.

Expanding the LED functionality

In order for the Raspberry Pi to know when to switch the LED on, we need to query the SQLite database, grab the temperature readings, and then decide whether the result warrants alerting us to a problem.

 To read from the database, we can use the example C++ code from the SQLite3 website, at http://www.sqlite.org/quickstart.html.

This code allows us to pass a query to the program. It will then execute the query and output the results. You can integrate the C++ code with your application by placing it in a separate method and removing any of the example code you do not need.

The functions we are most interested in are as follows:

- `sqlite3_open()` : This is responsible for opening the SQLite database connection
- `sqlite3_close()` : The close function closes an open database connection
- `sqlite3_exec()` : We use this function to execute a query

In order to grab the latest temperature data, you will need to use the following SQL query in your C++ code:

```
SELECT LAST(TemperatureC), LAST(Humidity) FROM Temperature;
```

Once we have the temperature and humidity values, we can add a calculation to check whether the value indicates dampness.

A simple activity would be to check whether the humidity is above a certain value, for example, 60 percent. If it is, we trigger the LED to switch on. We can modify the original blinking code in the following manner:

```
void loop() {

  if(damp) {
    digitalWrite(2,HIGH);
    delay(1000);
    digitalWrite(2,LOW);
    delay(1000);
  } else {
    digitalWrite(2, LOW);
  }
}
```

Here, we have a variable called `damp` that would need to be declared at the beginning of our application. This would be a Boolean variable that indicates that the value returned from the database is a cause of concern.

When the damp variable is set to `True`, we trigger the LED to flash. This variable can be set in the method you used to process the data returned from the database. You can now expand this code to include a method that can stop the LED flashing programmatically; for example, you can think of a way to switch it off once you have checked the damp situation.

Adding an LED alert is not the only modification we could make to the system. We could, for example, switch a dehumidifier on when the humidity is high to help address the problem. The next section explores this idea.

Connecting a dehumidifier

We now have a system that checks whether the humidity of a room is too high. It would be great if this system could also react to the data it receives and attempt to help solve the situation.

One method is to connect a dehumidifier and then switch it on when needed.

We could reuse the code from *Chapter 3, Central Air and Heating Thermostat*, and the relay module, and integrate them with our damp detection sketch. Taking this code, we would change the setpoint to a value representing humidity.

Next, we could check the humidity value read by the AM2302, and switch the relay on or off as needed.

For example, the code would be changed to use the h variable:

```
if(h >= setpoint) {
  digitalWrite(relay,HIGH);
} else {
  digitalWrite(relay,LOW);
}
```

As with the fan in *Chapter 3, Central Air and Heating Thermostat*, the next task would be to splice the wires on the dehumidifier and connect them to the relay module.

When the humidity rises above the setpoint, the relay will switch on and trigger the dehumidifier.

 Always remember to unplug devices when attaching them to the relay.

Now that we have a way to address damp issues using technologies we have already worked with, let's explore some other options to test for more severe problems.

Water detection

Of course, testing for humidity might not alert us to a major leak problem. During a severe rainstorm, the basement could be flooded quickly if it relies on a sump pump and that breaks down.

One device we could use with an Arduino or attach to the Raspberry Pi via the bridge shield is a water sensor.

Seed Studios offer such a device (`http://www.seeedstudio.com/depot/Grove-Water-Sensor-p-748.html`) that can be connected to either the analog or digital pins on your microcontroller.

With this device hooked up, the following example sketch can be run to check whether device is working correctly.

 The example sketch is available on GitHub, at `https://github.com/Seeed-Studio/Grove_Water_Sensor`.

Integrating this module with your existing damp detection circuit is simple. Attach the device to one of the digital pins on your Uno. Next, add the following code to your damp detection device sketch:

```
boolean waterDetected() {
  if(digitalRead(WATER_SENSOR) == LOW) {
     return true;
  } else {
    return false;
}
```

Here, the `WATER_SENSOR` variable is declared at the top of your sketch, and it references the pin that the device is connected to.

In the `loop()` function, we can call this method and then store the result in a variable, such as `water_detected`.

One possible approach would be to use the result in a modified version of the code that shows what the current temperature and humidity are:

```
client.println("Is water detected");
client.println(water_detected);
```

Once we have readings coming back from the sensor, there are a number of options on how we can be alerted to a water problem:

- We can reuse our e-mail code from *Chapter 5, Parcel Delivery Detector,* and have an alert sent directly to us.

- Integrate a buzzer. The GitHub code for the Grove water sensor demonstrates how a buzzer can be triggered when water is detected.

Buzzers can be found on Adafruit, at `http://www.adafruit.com/ products/160?gclid=CL-80ZqxjcMCFcli7Aod3BQA0g`.

- We can trigger the LED to blink. We do this by modifying the code from this chapter to enter in the database the information that flooding has been detected. Then our code makes the LED blink.

This wraps up the projects for this chapter. Let's revise what you've learned so far.

Summary

In this chapter, we explored a number of ways to detect damp and flooding. You were introduced to using the humidity functionality of the AM2302. Using this information, we wrote the humidity values to the database we created in *Chapter 4, Temperature Storage – Setting Up a Database to Store Your Results*.

Next, we used the Cooking Hacks shield to turn an LED on and off. Following this, we examined how we could use the LED to alert us about a dampness problem by checking the values stored in the database once an hour.

After building this system, we considered reusing the relay functionality from *Chapter 3, Central Air and Heating Thermostat*. This would then allow us to switch a dehumidifier on and off as needed.

Following this, we looked at a method of testing for water. This involved using a water sensor and modifying our code to send the concerned data back from the Arduino. Finally, we discussed a number of ways we could create an alert system to notify us that flooding could be taking place.

This completes the chapter, and hopefully, we have shown you how many of the technologies we introduced in earlier chapters can be combined to solve different problems. The next chapter will provide you with some ideas for future projects.

8
Wrapping Up

Throughout the previous chapters, we looked at various tools and technologies used to build devices that will help us automate our homes. The earlier chapters should have given you a good introduction to the Raspberry Pi and Arduino technologies, which you can now expand upon.

In this chapter, we will review what you've learned, and then look at how you can grow your skills and start designing your own shields for the Raspberry Pi.

We will look at a Raspberry Pi prototyping shield. Then we will explore the GPIO pins of the Raspberry Pi so that we can interact with them via the shield. Next, we will look at the `wiringPi` library and the Gertboard, both of which can be used for home automation projects. Furthermore, we will look at some projects that use the techniques you've learned in this book. In some cases, we will build upon previous projects. Finally, we wrap up with a look into the future.

In order to complete the prototype board task, you will need:

- The Raspberry Pi
- An Adafruit Raspberry Pi prototyping shield
- An LED
- A soldering iron
- Protective glasses
- Solder

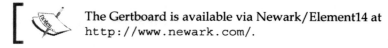 The Gertboard is available via Newark/Element14 at http://www.newark.com/.

Let's start by revising what we have covered so far.

A brief review of the second edition of Raspberry Pi Home Automation with Arduino

Those of you who read the first edition of this book may have noticed some changes. We hope these have provided you with some new and exciting projects. For first time readers, we hope these changes have whetted your appetite for learning more.

Here is an overview of the topics covered in each chapter, with some of the differences from the first edition:

Chapter 1, An Introduction to the Raspberry Pi, Arduino, and Home Automation, and *Chapter 2, Getting Started – Setting Up Your Raspberry Pi and Arduino*, provided you with some background on the Raspberry Pi, Arduino, and the Cooking Hacks shield. We saw that we can take a third-party shield and attach it to the Raspberry Pi. This provided us with the ability to control devices hooked up to the shield (via the Raspberry Pi's GPIO pins), as we would with an Arduino microcontroller. In the second edition of the book, we looked at the Arduino in more detail, and this helped us to pave the way for projects in later chapters.

Chapter 3, Central Air and Heating Thermostat, covered connecting devices via a breadboard to our Arduino. We covered sketches that leverage this data and prepared the Arduino to accept HTTP requests to output the data collected. Unlike the first edition of the book, the thermostat here was built with an Arduino Uno.

Following this, in *Chapter 4, Temperature Storage – Setting Up a Database to Store Your Results*, we set up our Raspberry Pi to query the Arduino thermostat and store temperature data in a SQLite database. The second edition of this book saw this chapter simplified so that more time could be spent writing Python code, and less in setting up web servers.

Chapter 5, Parcel Delivery Detector, built upon the previous chapter by walking us through building an Arduino parcel detector that writes data to the Raspberry Pi. This chapter introduced new components not seen in the first edition and also provided the opportunity to work with the Arduino further.

Chapter 6, Curtain Automation – Open and Close the Curtains Based on the Ambient Light, brought together some of our techniques from the earlier chapters. Like the first edition, it introduced us to the bridge shield and demonstrated controlling a DC motor using an Arduino motor shield.

Finally, *Chapter 7, Water/Damp Detection – Check for Damp/Flooding in Sheds and Basements*, showed you how to use a Cooking Hacks bridge shield to build a device that checks for flooding or dampness. This was a new chapter in this edition of the book, and introduced you to components we had not used in the first edition.

You should see from this review that you have slowly built up a set of techniques that use similar ideas but are transferable to devices that have different applications at home.

We can now use these methods to build custom devices.

Next steps

We have refreshed ourselves on the subjects covered so far. Let's look at future projects that you can try. These will provide you with a few ideas on how you can expand existing projects and provide some starting points to build your own ideas from scratch.

First, we'll review the prototyping Pi Plate. Then we will look at the Gertboard and its background. Finally, we'll provide some ideas for future projects that could use the Cooking Hacks shield, Gertboard, Arduino or the prototype shield.

The prototyping Pi Plate

The Raspberry Pi prototyping Pi Plate shield is a kit provided by Adafruit Industries. You can find out more about it at `http://learn.adafruit.com/adafruit-prototyping-pi-plate/overview`. It allows you to create a prototyping shield that connects to the GPIO pins on the Raspberry Pi. You may be familiar with this principle from the Cooking Hacks shield, which you used to build your previous projects. Unlike the Raspberry Pi to Arduino shield, this is a kit whose components need to be soldered together. By building this shield, you will get a platform that you can use for custom projects.

The prototyping Pi Plate consists of a single board divided between perfboard-style and breadboard-style pins.

Access to the Raspberry Pi GPIO pins is around the edge of board, where a number of screw terminals are fixed and *doubled* up with standard pins located further in on the board. The shield allows you to solder individual components to it and also place a miniature breadboard between the screw terminals for prototyping.

Using an example from *Chapter 6, Curtain Automation – Open and Close the Curtains Based on the Ambient Light*, we can solder our components directly to the prototype shield, and thus have a compact device that uses a single shield.

A comprehensive guide to soldering the shield can be found at
`http://learn.adafruit.com/adafruit-prototyping-pi-`
`plate/solder-it.`
Remember to use protective eyewear while soldering to avoid
risk of injury to your eyes. Also make sure you solder in a well-
ventilated area.

Let's look at the GPIO pin arrangement and naming convention on the Raspberry Pi
so that you can cross-reference these with the prototyping Pi Plate when you wire up
your projects. This layout is based upon looking at the Raspberry Pi with the GPIO
pins located at the top-right corner of the board.

The schematic at `https://www.adafruit.com/datasheets/`
`pi2schem.pdf` may also help you.

The pins are located in two columns, with each pin labeled with its role; for example,
location 1 is the 3.3V pin.

You will notice that a number of these are labeled as **Not used**. These
pins are currently not used and are set aside for future expansions of
the Raspberry Pi's architecture.

With this information, we can write custom code to interact with the pins, or use
other generic libraries that allow us to read and write data. The `wiringPi` library,
which we will now look at, provides a few software tools that we can use with our
Raspberry Pi Plate.

The wiringPi library

The `wiringPi` library, written by Gordon Henderson, interacts with the Raspberry
Pi in a fashion similar to the `arduPi` library. It provides an alternative to the software
library you are currently using, and it can be explored for future projects, such as
extending the functionality of your curtain automation device.

In the `wiringPi` library, you will find not only support for the many Arduino
functions that you are familiar with, but also custom support for PWM.

A comprehensive guide to the available functions is accessible on the wiringPi webpage, at http://wiringpi.com/.

The download and installation instructions for this library can be found at http://wiringpi.com/download-and-install/.

Once the installation is complete, there are a number of examples you can try out. One of them that may be of interest to you is test2.c in the example directory. This program simulates PWM, and if you connect an LED to pin 2, you will see the LED slowly fade on and off.

The prototyping Pi Plate and wiringPi library provide you with an interesting alternative to the Cooking Hacks shield. Let's now look at another technology that is available for the Raspberry Pi — the Gertboard.

The Gertboard

The Gertboard is a device that connects to the Raspberry Pi's GPIO pins, as we have seen with the previous shields. It provides the user with a variety of tools to interact with electronic components. The Gertboard was developed by and named after Gert Van Loo.

Gert Van Loo, while working with Ebon Upton at Broadcom took up the challenge of building a stripped-down computer. Using a multimedia-optimized processor, the BCM2835, he developed the prototype of the Raspberry Pi's alpha hardware.

Following the success of the Raspberry Pi, he worked on a project that would further expand what the Raspberry Pi could do — the Gertboard. This is a **printed circuit board (PCB)** with a combination of components that can be soldered together and connected to the Raspberry Pi, thus extending its capabilities via its GPIO pins. Like its counterparts, the Gertboard allows electronic components to be controlled via applications written on the Raspberry Pi.

While not an official product of the Raspberry Pi Foundation, it has been given support by its members and distributed alongside the Raspberry Pi through Newark/Element 14.

Much like the Raspberry Pi to Arduino shield, you will now be able to build embedded systems for your home that can perform a range of tasks, from recording temperatures and controlling your thermostat to using ambient light sensors that open and close your blinds.

Thanks to the combination of components that come as part of the kit, you will have sensors, LEDS, DACS, and motors available for home projects. These allow you to record analog data and convert it to digital information, as well as move physical objects via motors and communicate error codes and states via LEDs.

Introduction to the Gertboard components

The first wave of Gertboards was shipped as a kit of separate components that needed to be soldered together. Subsequently, an updated prebuilt kit was released. The kit and pre-soldered board includes the following components:

- Buttons
- A GPIO PCB board
- A ribbon cable
- LEDs
- Analog to digital convertor
- Digital to analog convertor
- A 48V motor controller
- An ATmega microcontroller

Let's now take a look at what each of these items does.

GPIO PCB expansion board

The GPIO expansion board is a prepopulated PCB. This is the item to which the components are soldered, and it forms the foundation of the Gertboard. This board is connected to the Raspberry Pi via its GPIO pins.

GPIO pins

The Gertboard, like the Raspberry Pi, comes equipped with its own set of GPIO pins. The ribbon cable provided in the Gertboard kit is used to hook up the Raspberry Pi to some of the GPIO pins in order to provide a physical medium of communication between the two devices.

Motor controller

A motor controller can be used to control an electronic motor hooked up to it. Some examples of its functionality include switching a motor on and off, controlling its speed, and changing its torque and direction.

The Gertboard's motor controller supports hooking up a **direct current** (DC) electric motor, which can be controlled via the motor controller's pins. It also comes equipped with a fuse for current protection and internal temperature protection to help prevent overheating. This removes the need to use a separate motor shield as we did in *Chapter 6, Curtain Automation – Open and Close the Curtains Based on the Ambient Light*.

The open collector drivers

The **open collector drivers** (OC drivers) are used to turn the devices that are connected to the Gertboard on and off. This is especially useful when the device connected requires a higher voltage than what is available via the Gertboard.

One common application of the OC drivers is to hook up the devices used to display visual data, such as a **Vacuum fluorescent display** (VFD). These are the types of display that you may commonly find in home appliances such as your cooker or microwave. They are used to communicate information such as cooking time and temperature.

Buffered I/O

The input/output ports on the Gertboard are where you will connect your buttons and LEDs. These are controlled via jumpers, which set the port to input or output mode.

The button, for example, is an input mechanism, and the LED is an output mechanism. Switching an LED on will result in sending the command from the Raspberry Pi via an output to the Gertboard as an input.

A pushbutton works in an opposite way to this, whereby an input from the button is sent to the Gertboard, and an output from the Gertboard is received as an input to the Raspberry Pi.

While using jumpers, it is important to think of the above in the following terms. An input jumper means an input to the Raspberry Pi, and an output jumper means an output from the Raspberry Pi.

Atmel ATmega microcontroller

The Atmel ATmega microcontroller device is the microcontroller for the Gertboard. The microcontroller is a single, integrated computer that controls the input and output of the devices on the Gertboard.

The development language for Arduino can be used with the Gertboard (because the Arduino is also based on the ATmega series of microcontrollers). Once you have this installed, you can reuse Arduino-specific applications with a few changes or write new ones to control the Gertboard's microcontroller.

Convertors – analog to digital and digital to analog

ADC and DAC are used to convert data from one format to another. They have seen applications in music recording and videos. They are also useful for converting analog readings from thermostats to digital readings.

For those interested in a more in-depth look at the Gertboard, the user manual is available at the Element14 website. This manual provides an in-depth look at the electronic components that come as parts of the kit, and is available at http://www.element14.com/community/servlet/JiveServlet/downloadBody/51727-102-3-267366/Gertboard_UM_final_with_schematics.pdf.

Creating software for the Gertboard

There are several example programs written for the Gertboard in C that you may be interested in checking out, at http://www.element14.com/community/docs/DOC-61025/1/gertboard-application-library-for-gertboard-kit-linux.

Gordon Henderson's website also provides a guide to install the Arduino IDE on the Raspberry Pi and configure it to work with the Gertboard. The instructions can be found at https://projects.drogon.net/raspberry-pi/gertboard/arduino-ide-installation-isp/.

So, with two new boards to explore and some different libraries, let's look at some future projects that can leverage your existing hardware (an Arduino microcontroller) or use one of the other shields we have looked at.

Ideas for future projects

This book includes a variety of projects that provide tools to sense and automate your home environment. Armed with knowledge after completing these projects, you are now equipped with the skills to expand your existing projects and create exciting new devices. The following is list that provides some potential projects for the future.

Expanding the curtain automation tool to include temperature sensing

Your current application from *Chapter 6, Curtain Automation – Open and Close the Curtains Based on the Ambient Light*, uses light to decide when to open and close the blinds or curtains. You can now try combining the thermostat from *Chapter 3, Central Air and Heating Thermostat*, with the curtain control device and redevelop the software to incorporate temperature data. Using the thermistor, you can decide to open and close your blinds according to temperature changes in order to conserve heat.

By expanding the database written in *Chapter 4, Temperature Storage – Setting Up a Database to Store Your Results*, we can also record the time when the curtains are opened or closed, to give us an idea of how many hours of sunlight we received across a day in a certain month of the year.

This project would need no components other than those used in *Chapter 4, Temperature Storage – Setting Up a Database to Store Your Results*, and *Chapter 6, Curtain Automation – Open and Close the Curtains Based on the Ambient Light*.

Changing the motor on the curtain automation project to a stepper motor

We are currently using a small DC motor in *Chapter 6, Curtain Automation – Open and Close the Curtains Based on the Ambient Light*, in order to control the blinds in the project. We can replace the regular DC motor with a DC stepper motor as we suggested at the end of that chapter.

A stepper motor is a motor that divides a full revolution into *steps*. This allows greater control over the revolutions of the motor while it is operating, and thus, greater accuracy in controlling the drawstring. Attaching multiple stepper motors to your device will allow you to control multiple blinds in a room.

Switching lights on with a photoresistor

You have learned how to switch on a fan using relays and a thermistor. The principles used in this project can be applied to a desktop lamp or a similar lighting device. Using the relay shield, an Arduino Uno, and a photoresistor, we can write an application to switch on the lighting device when the room gets dark.

Holiday lights from LEDs

One application of the PWM code we wrote in *Chapter 6, Curtain Automation – Open and Close the Curtains Based on the Ambient Light*, is to cause LEDs to blink on and off. This provides us with the technology to make holiday lights that can blink and fade in a pattern. To build this project, you can time the lights to switch on and off in synchronization with music to provide an even more interesting experience.

The future of home automation

The Raspberry Pi and Arduino are two great technologies to create home automation projects. As they continue to grow, the tasks that we will be able to achieve at home using homebrew devices will grow even larger.

Let's take a look of some of the other tools that will become increasingly available to home enthusiasts.

3D printing

3D printing is a method of taking a three-dimensional image and then printing it in a substance such as plastic or metal. The advent of cheaper 3D printing has provided home automation enthusiasts with a new tool for their arsenal. 3D printing's ability to create custom cases and brackets for devices, and then print these in plastic provides a gateway to a whole new world of exciting designs.

Printers such as the Makerbot have opened up 3D printing to the home market. For those who can't afford a 3D printer at home, there are services such as Shapeways (http://www.shapeways.com/), which allows the customer to upload a 3D image to the website. Shapeways will take this 3D image, print the object in a variety of materials, and then ship it. Also, Raspberry Pi cases are a popular offer on their website!

RFID chips

Radio Frequency Identification (RFID) is a method where microchips are embedded in items such as passports. When these chips are read, they provide the information encoded in them.

Consumer goods are increasingly approaching the realm where embedded RFID chips will become commonplace. When this takes place, home automation devices will be able to read the frequencies of products that enter the house and leave. Thus, a system can be built to read signals and add to an inventory the groceries you have brought home.

With respect to throwing out the empty cans and packaging, the inventory system will be able to track these leaving the kitchen and remove them from the database.

Therefore, inventory management of goods in the home will become an almost seamless process.

EEG headsets

EEG headsets are devices that allow people to interact with their computers through thought. This sounds like something from science fiction. However, products such as the Emotiv headset (http://www.emotiv.com) and the Interaxon Muse (http://www.choosemuse.com/) are carving the way for home EEG devices.

As software becomes widespread for EEG devices, it will only be a matter of time before home automation projects are touched by this technology.

The ability to think the lights on is going to provide home automation enthusiasts with a plenty of exciting projects. A benefit of this will also be for those with disabilities, who will be provided with ways to interact with their home.

With technologies such as these on the horizon, we believe there will be many great opportunities to leverage the power of the Raspberry Pi and many exciting projects for enthusiasts such as you.

Summary

The Raspberry Pi and Arduino platforms are inexpensive computers with a lot of potential. By choosing these technologies, you have provided yourself with a fantastic tool set to build home automation projects.

In this book, we aimed to provide you with examples that are useful and slowly build up in difficulty, expanding your knowledge of the Raspberry Pi, Arduino, Linux, and related technologies along the way.

Our projects covered the application of the Raspberry Pi in home automation, and showed you how you can leverage the existing Arduino toolset to augment the Raspberry Pi's abilities. As newer and more powerful versions are released, we believe the future for this technology is, indeed, very bright.

The Raspberry Pi community is growing by the day, and the best place to share your projects and look for help is at the Raspberry Pi website forum, at http://www.raspberrypi.org/forums/.

The Arduino community is well established and, like the Raspberry Pi website, has a lively forum where you can ask for help, at http://arduino.cc/forum/.

We started the book by looking at the history of home automation, and finished it by looking at the future.

With this information, it is now over to you, to continue your journey.

References

In this appendix, we will be seeing some links and resources that will be useful for you for future projects, and will help you to learn more about the technologies used in this book.

These links cover a variety of sites, including commercial and open source. You will also find URLs that provide additional information on some of the commands and programming languages that we have used. Let's look at them one by one.

Raspberry Pi

The following links provide information and support for the Raspberry Pi and Raspbian operating system:

- Official Raspberry Pi website: http://www.raspberrypi.org/
- Official Raspberry Pi forum: http://www.raspberrypi.org/phpBB3/
- Raspbian website: http://www.raspbian.org/
- The wiringPi library: http://wiringpi.com/
- Gertboard user manual: http://www.element14.com/community/servlet/JiveServlet/downloadBody/51727-102-3-267366/Gertboard_UM_final_with_schematics.pdf
- eLinux Raspberry Pi Hub: http://elinux.org/RPi_Hub

Raspberry Pi to Arduino bridge shield

Information on the Cooking Hacks Raspberry Pi to Arduino bridge can be found at these links:

- Cooking Hacks website: `http://www.cooking-hacks.com/`

- Raspberry Pi to Arduino tutorial: `http://www.cooking-hacks.com/index.php/documentation/tutorials/raspberry-pi-to-arduino-shields-connection-bridge`

- The `arduPi` library board revision 1: `http://www.cooking-hacks.com/skin/frontend/default/cooking/images/catalog/documentation/raspberry_arduino_shield/arduPi_rev1.tar.gz`

- The `arduPi` library board revision 2: `http://www.cooking-hacks.com/skin/frontend/default/cooking/images/catalog/documentation/raspberry_arduino_shield/arduPi_rev2.tar.gz`

Linux

There is a wide range of resources available for Linux online as well as via the Linux `man` command. The following links provide overviews of commands and packages used in this book:

- User's manual for `screen`:
  `http://www.gnu.org/software/screen/manual/screen.html`

- Raspbian package information: `http://elinux.org/Raspbian`

- User manual for `apt-get`: `http://linux.die.net/man/8/apt-get`

- User manual for `wget`:
  `http://www.gnu.org/software/wget/manual/wget.html`

- Linux Kernel archive: `http://www.kernel.org/`

- Geany IDE: `http://www.geany.org/`

- Command manual for `make`: `http://linux.die.net/man/1/make`

- Manual page for `chmod`: `http://linux.die.net/man/1/chmod`

- Manual page for `chown`: `http://linux.die.net/man/1/chown`

Python

Various Python resources that are useful to you, including information on the WSGI technology, are available at these links:

- Official Python website: http://www.python.org/
- Python documentation: http://docs.python.org/
- WSGI homepage: http://www.wsgi.org/
- Python pip: http://pypi.python.org/pypi/pip
- Downloading Python: http://www.python.org/getit/

C/C++

The following collection of links provides you with further information on the C and C++ programming languages:

- C and C++ programming reference: http://www.cprogramming.com/
- POSIX threads: https://computing.llnl.gov/tutorials/pthreads/
- G++ compiler: http://linux.die.net/man/1/g++

Arduino

We have provided some useful resources on the Arduino hardware and software that you can use to explore this open source technology:

- Official Arduino homepage: http://www.arduino.cc/
- Official Arduino forum: http://arduino.cc/forum/
- Official Arduino store: http://store.arduino.cc/
- Arduino IDE downloads: http://arduino.cc/en/Main/Software
- Arduino hardware: http://arduino.cc/en/Main/Products?from=Main.Hardware
- Makezine's Arduino blog: http://blog.makezine.com/arduino/

SQL

There are a variety of flavors of SQL. The following URLs are geared towards SQLite, which we used in this book for our temperature storage database:

- SQLite homepage: `http://www.sqlite.org/`
- SQLite downloads: `http://www.sqlite.org/download.html`
- SQLite Documentation: `http://www.sqlite.org/docs.html`
- W3 Schools SQL guide: `http://www.w3schools.com/sql/default.asp`

HTSQL

Here are the links that contain in-depth coverage of the HTSQL query language. Using these reference guides, you can expand the complexity of the queries you write for your home automation projects:

- Official HTSQL website: `http://htsql.org/`
- HTSQL tutorial: `http://htsql.org/doc/tutorial.html`
- HTSQL downloads: `http://htsql.org/download/`
- HTSQL Python page: `http://pypi.python.org/pypi/HTSQL`
- HTSQL mailing list:
  `http://lists.htsql.org/mailman/listinfo/htsql-users`

Electronics

You can order the electronic components online from a variety of sources. These URLs are for major suppliers who stock the components used in this book. We have also provided some links to the basic electronic guides:

- Adafruit industries: `http://www.adafruit.com/`
- Cooking Hacks: `http://www.cooking-hacks.com/`
- Makeshed: `http://www.makershed.com/`
- Element14: `http://www.element14.com/`
- RS Components: `http://www.rs-components.com`
- Wikipedia article on electronic symbols: `http://en.wikipedia.org/wiki/Electronic_symbol`

Packt Publishing titles

Packt Publishing offers a variety of books on many of the technologies used in this book. We have provided links to titles that may interest you:

- Packt Publishing homepage: `http://www.packtpub.com/`

- *Expert Python Programming*: `http://www.packtpub.com/expert-python-programming/book`

- *Linux Shell Scripting Cookbook*: `http://www.packtpub.com/linux-shell-scripting-cookbook/book-0`

- *CherryPy Essentials: Rapid Python Web Application development*: `http://www.packtpub.com/CherryPy/book`

Home automation technology

For those interested in commercial and open source home automation applications and technology, we have provided links to several resources, including those related to X10:

- X10 knowledge base: `http://kbase.x10.com/wiki/Main_Page`

- X10.com: `http://www.x10.com/homepage.htm`

- Nest Learning Thermostat: `http://www.nest.com/`

- Android operating system: `http://www.android.com/`

- Android developer resources: `http://developer.android.com/index.html`

- Open source automation (Windows-based): `http://www.opensourceautomation.com/`

- Open Remote: `http://www.openremote.org/display/HOME/OpenRemote`

- Honeywell for your home: `http://yourhome.honeywell.com/home/`

- Hackaday blog: `http://hackaday.com/`

- Iris Smart Kit: `http://www.lowes.com/cd_Products_1337707661000_`

3D printing

3D printing provides home automation enthusiasts with the tools that they can use to build custom cases, brackets, gears, and other tools for their systems. The following links cover 3D printers and 3D printing services:

- Makerbot 3D printers: `http://www.makerbot.com/`
- Thingiverse: `http://www.thingiverse.com/`
- Shapeways 3D printing on demand: `http://www.shapeways.com/`
- Stratasys 3D printers: `http://www.stratasys.com/`
- i.materialise: `http://i.materialise.com/`
- Next Engine 3D scanner: `http://www.nextengine.com/`
- David 3D scanner: `http://www.david-laserscanner.com/`

Here is a list of miscellaneous resources based on some of the topics touched upon in this book, and other areas of interest:

- *Popular mechanics* back issues at Google Books: `http://books.google.com/books?id=49gDAAAAMBAJ&source=gbs_all_issues_r&cad=1&atm_aiy=1960#all_issues_anchor`
- Wikipedia article on mains electricity: `http://en.wikipedia.org/wiki/Mains_electricity`
- Wikipedia article on relays: `http://en.wikipedia.org/wiki/Relay`
- Wikibooks content on embedded systems: `http://en.wikibooks.org/wiki/Embedded_Systems`
- Open Source Initiative: `http://opensource.org/`

Index

Thank you for buying
Raspberry Pi Home Automation with Arduino
Second Edition

About Packt Publishing

Packt, pronounced 'packed', published its first book, *Mastering phpMyAdmin for Effective MySQL Management*, in April 2004, and subsequently continued to specialize in publishing highly focused books on specific technologies and solutions.

Our books and publications share the experiences of your fellow IT professionals in adapting and customizing today's systems, applications, and frameworks. Our solution-based books give you the knowledge and power to customize the software and technologies you're using to get the job done. Packt books are more specific and less general than the IT books you have seen in the past. Our unique business model allows us to bring you more focused information, giving you more of what you need to know, and less of what you don't.

Packt is a modern yet unique publishing company that focuses on producing quality, cutting-edge books for communities of developers, administrators, and newbies alike. For more information, please visit our website at www.packtpub.com.

About Packt Open Source

In 2010, Packt launched two new brands, Packt Open Source and Packt Enterprise, in order to continue its focus on specialization. This book is part of the Packt Open Source brand, home to books published on software built around open source licenses, and offering information to anybody from advanced developers to budding web designers. The Open Source brand also runs Packt's Open Source Royalty Scheme, by which Packt gives a royalty to each open source project about whose software a book is sold.

Writing for Packt

We welcome all inquiries from people who are interested in authoring. Book proposals should be sent to author@packtpub.com. If your book idea is still at an early stage and you would like to discuss it first before writing a formal book proposal, then please contact us; one of our commissioning editors will get in touch with you.

We're not just looking for published authors; if you have strong technical skills but no writing experience, our experienced editors can help you develop a writing career, or simply get some additional reward for your expertise.

[PACKT]
PUBLISHING

open source *
community experience distilled

Raspberry Pi Home Automation with Arduino

ISBN: 978-1-84969-586-2   Paperback: 176 pages

Automate your home with a set of exciting projects for the Raspberry Pi!

1. Learn how to dynamically adjust your living environment with detailed step-by-step examples.

2. Discover how you can utilize the combined power of the Raspberry Pi and Arduino for your own projects.

3. Revolutionize the way you interact with your home on a daily basis.

Arduino Home Automation Projects

ISBN: 978-1-78398-606-4   Paperback: 132 pages

Automate your home using the powerful Arduino platform

1. Interface home automation components with Arduino.

2. Automate your projects to communicate wirelessly using XBee, Bluetooth and WiFi.

3. Build seven exciting, instruction-based home automation projects with Arduino in no time.

Please check **www.PacktPub.com** for information on our titles

Raspberry Pi Cookbook for Python Programmers

ISBN: 978-1-84969-662-3   Paperback: 402 pages

Over 50 easy-to-comprehend tailor-made recipes to get the most out of the Raspberry Pi and unleash its huge potential using Python

1. Install your first operating system, share files over the network, and run programs remotely.

2. Unleash the hidden potential of the Raspberry Pi's powerful Video Core IV graphics processor with your own hardware accelerated 3D graphics.

3. Discover how to create your own electronic circuits to interact with the Raspberry Pi.

Raspberry Pi for Secret Agents

ISBN: 978-1-84969-578-7   Paperback: 152 pages

Turn your Raspberry Pi into your very own secret agent toolbox with this set of exciting projects!

1. Detect an intruder on camera and set off an alarm.

2. Listen in or record conversations from a distance.

3. Find out what the other computers on your network are up to.

4. Unleash your Raspberry Pi on the world.

Please check **www.PacktPub.com** for information on our titles

CPSIA information can be obtained
at www.ICGtesting.com
Printed in the USA
LVOW09s1726251116

514460LV00005B/206/P